From a very early age, Joanne Hull has had an affinity with animals. During her childhood she discovered that her natural psychic ability gave her a connection with animals that was much more intense than she ever imagined possible. Now a TV favourite after her appearances on *The Wright Stuff* and the *Sharon Osbourne Show*, her gift has helped thousands of people connect with their pets past and present. Joanne currently lives in Scotland with her fiancé, Fraser.

Joanne Hull

headline

First published in 2010
by HEADLINE PUBLISHING GROUP

1

Cataloguing in Publication Data is available from the British Library

ISBN 978 0 7553 1971 8

Typeset by Palimpsest Book Production Limited,
Grangemouth, Stirlingshire

Printed and bound in Great Britain by
Clays Ltd, St Ives plc

Headline's policy is to use papers that are natural, renewable and recyclable
products and made from wood grown in sustainable forests. The logging and
manufacturing processes are expected to conform to the
environmental regulations of the country of origin.

HEADLINE PUBLISHING GROUP
An Hachette UK Company
338 Euston Road
London NW1 3BH

www.headline.co.uk
www.hachette.co.uk
www.joannehull.com

This book is dedicated to the animals.

Author's note

The decision to write this book was one of the hardest I have ever made: in writing it I embarked upon an emotional journey. Reliving memories isn't always easy, and learning about who I am became a real eye-opener (who needs a therapist?). But I'm glad to say that, all things considered, I wouldn't change a thing.

Names have been changed to protect the innocent.

Although I use the word 'owners' throughout this book, my belief is not that we own our animals, but that we share our lives with them.

I pour another cup of coffee and settle down at my desk with Oshan, my cat, waiting eagerly for my computer's mouse to start moving. I try to explain to him it's not a real mouse but, being a house cat, he doesn't seem to grasp this notion. Sipping my coffee, with Oshan purring excitedly by my side, we get set for another magical encounter with the animals. My life is certainly not ordinary; sometimes I have to pinch myself to make sure that I've not just dreamed it. I have been entrusted with a gift – an incredible ability to communicate with animals.

When I reflect on my life, it's clear to me that every twist and turn, through the good and the bad, has led me to where I am today, and boy, am I so very grateful! At the age of thirty-eight, I still feel like the ordinary little girl from Bedworth I once was, even after all the extraordinary things I've seen and experienced. And I sincerely believe that I have the most amazing life still to come. Each animal I meet is so very special and I see every day as a gift and a new beginning. I look forward to my future. I am truly blessed.

Every day, people send me photographs of animals to read, and my day usually begins with collecting the latest photographs from my post box. The animals could be anything from household pets, like dogs and cats, to horses, cattle or even wild creatures. Some have already passed over to spirit, whilst others are still alive. I have no previous connection with most of the animals I work with. I never know what I am going to get from day to day – sometimes it's sad, sometimes it's happy – and this makes my work very special.

The picture I've been asked to work with today is of a little Jack Russell named Peanut. Owners usually have a list of questions for me to ask their animals, but this time it was different. The owner of Peanut only wanted to ask one. Yep, just one, and this was it . . . 'Do you forgive me?'

Peanut's owner felt an enormous amount of guilt about Peanut's passing, since she'd been away on a business trip to Jersey when Peanut went to spirit. Like so many other people I've read for in that position, her owner could not shake off the heartache of not having been with her little dog at the end of her life. After all, her dog had always been at her side during her most difficult and trying times.

Peanut's owner's words sent a chill through my body as I turned my focus to the little orange and white dog in the photo. She had eyes as golden as sand, with a beautiful nose as black as coal. What an amazing little dog you are, I thought, as I stared down at her image. My heart began to beat faster, and my fingers tingled with excitement as I could feel the connection I like to call the 'love link'. This happens when two hearts achieve such closeness that they almost become one. Peanut and I were in tune. If it helps you imagine it, think of the moment when you're searching through crackling static and muffled voices for a particular radio station and then you suddenly find the right channel. Unconditional love swept over my entire body and I sensed Peanut had passed to spirit.

I began to think about the question her owner wanted to ask, but before I could even utter the words, 'Do you forgive her?', Peanut began to speak through me. Animals can communicate with me in a number of different ways. Sometime they send me a picture, sometimes moving images (a bit like a video) but in Peanut's case the message came through as a voice connection. The animals don't speak to me in their own voice; what I hear is a voice similar to my own but subtly altered by each animal's personality, which I pick up on as I translate what they have to say. It's sensing these personality traits that lets me know I'm listening to a dog, and not to myself!

Peanut's message was loud and clear for me to understand. 'Please tell my mum that I am OK now. I have no pain, and enjoy my walks again. There's nothing I need to forgive her for. I didn't need her with me when I passed to spirit. I have left my love for her under the red rose bush in the front garden.'

And with that the little orange and white dog was gone. The link I'd formed with her had been broken in an instant. I was shocked at how quickly Peanut had connected with me, but also how brief her message was. I didn't feel I had a lot to tell her owner, but hoped those few words would give her some comfort all the same.

I dialled Peanut's owner's telephone number and waited for her to pick up at the other end. I always get nervous at this point, I'm not really sure why. Perhaps I'm worried that I may have got something wrong, or that the owner will be disappointed with what I have to tell them. I remind myself that I am just a channel for information and I have to trust what the animals tell me. All I can do is pass on what I hear to the owner and cross my fingers that it will help. Still, every case is different, and you can never guess how people will react.

'Hello, it's Joanne here,' I said when Peanut's owner answered.

'Ah yes, Joanne. Did you manage to speak with Peanut?' she asked, sounding nervous, as if she was wondering what I was going to say.

'Yep, short and sweet,' I laughed, speaking in a soft voice to reassure her. 'Peanut said she is fine and well and enjoys her walks now. She didn't feel the need for forgiveness and she said to tell you she has left you her love under the red rose bush in the front garden.'

Peanut's owner sounded almost overcome with emotion. She thanked me breathlessly and asked me to stay on the line as she went with her phone still in her hand to investigate the rose bush in the front garden.

That's a good start, I thought to myself. At least she has a rose bush! I've lost count of the number of readings I've done for people, but I've never stopped being relieved when it begins to sound as if what I've said is being validated, still better that it might be helping someone.

As I held the handset to my ear I could hear the faint sounds of her walking up the garden path, then stopping. There was a moment of silence before I was almost deafened by a cry coming straight down the phone line.

'Are you OK?' I asked, slightly concerned.

'Oh, Joanne, Peanut has left her love for me!' she said.

'What do you mean?' I asked.

'Just before Peanut died, I gave her a soft toy. It was a small, dark red velvet heart with the word LOVE sewn onto the front of it. I told her I would always love her. Here under the bush is the heart. It's Peanut's velvet heart!' her owner exclaimed in a flood of tears.

At that moment I felt like the luckiest person alive. Both of us wept as we celebrated Peanut's life. Her owner told me how Peanut had developed terminal cancer, but also started to laugh as she remembered her little quirks, her funny tricks and her dumpy little legs. And she described how Peanut's love and support had helped her when she felt at her lowest during her traumatic divorce. 'Nothing can compare to my little Peanut, but I was worried that she never knew how much I loved her, how thankful I was that I had such a loyal friend. When she fell ill there was nothing I could do to help except watch her fade away. That's why I wanted to speak to you, so I could make sure she didn't feel I'd let her down after she'd done so much for me.'

It's stories like this that prove to me I really can make a difference. I know people will often say 'It's just a dog' or 'It's only a cat', but I and many others know better. These wonderful, intelligent creatures know and feel more than we will probably ever give them credit for. Animals deserve to be heard, deserve to be understood and, most importantly, deserve to be loved.

Chapter One

On a cold winter's day in 1971, my mother Jean, pregnant with me, suggested to my father that the family bought a dog. He was doubtful, to say the least. It wasn't that my dad didn't like dogs – in fact, he adored them – but he thought my mum already had enough on her plate, what with looking after the house and three small children. However, my mother's patience and persuasiveness eventually paid off, my father's reluctance was overcome and the search for a small dog began.

A few weeks went by before a knock at our door produced two police officers. Unsurprisingly, my mum was startled at first, fearing that they were bringing bad news.

'Mrs Hull?' asked the taller and thinner of the two.

'Yes,' she replied, still anxious.

'We heard your husband was looking for a dog,' the other officer said. (To this day, my mother still talks about the well-trimmed moustache, carefully groomed into a curl at each end, he was sporting.)

'Yes.'

'Do you want this one?'

With that the policeman pointed to a dog in the back of his car. My mother followed his gaze and saw a black, very sad-looking medium-sized mongrel staring back at her. It was nothing like what Mum and Dad had in mind for the family. For one thing, he was at least double the size they were looking for, and for another, Mum had set her heart on something cute and fluffy, which this dog certainly wasn't. But, looking through that car window at his sad face and kind eyes, my mum instantly fell in love with him. She felt a connection like no other. It was clear to her that the dog needed her as much as she needed him. The mournful-faced dog sitting inside the police car now had a place he could call home.

When my dad came back from work that evening he was surprised to be welcomed by a strange black figure wagging his tail. Mum explained what had happened and later, after the children had gone to bed, both my parents sat down to think of a name for their new addition. After much deliberation, and with numerous alternatives considered then tossed aside, they decided to call him Blackie (well, he was black, after all). And so he became our dog Blackie.

Though Blackie seemed happy to be around us on that first day, Mum couldn't help noticing that he kept staring at the door, almost as if he needed to be somewhere else. It soon turned out that Mum's instincts were right. Blackie had only been with our family for a day when my mum let him into the back garden to do his business. He began sniffing around the rhubarb patch that Dad had covered with chicken wire the previous night to protect his pride and joy. Just then my sister Janice called out from the kitchen asking for a glass of fizzy cola, and with my mother's attention elsewhere for a few minutes, Blackie took the chance to sneak under the garden fence and escape at full speed up the road, swiftly disappearing into the distance.

When she realised he was gone my mum panicked. Blackie had only just joined the family and she wanted him to be happy with us. The last thing she wanted was to lose him.

Being pregnant and having three young children to look after, Mum couldn't go out and search for him but she had taken the police officer's telephone number. At the time we didn't have a telephone in the house, so she shouted over the garden fence to our neighbour. Betty was a small stout woman, with a big friendly smile and lips that were always dressed with orange lip stain. Her tightly curled auburn hair was kept neatly in place by a brown-coloured hair net. She didn't have any children of her own and often helped with the three youngsters, keeping an eye on them so Mum could get the chores done. As happy to help as always, Betty went to the local telephone box to report Blackie as missing.

To Mum's relief, Betty's phone call worked. Just a few hours later, Blackie was returned safe and sound by the police officers. Delighted as she was to have him home, she didn't think to ask the officers where they'd found him. Mum recalls Blackie being a little distressed after his return. He wouldn't settle, and kept looking out of the front room window. He would lie down in front of the fire to relax, but then just as he was about to close his eyes, he would suddenly jump up and stare again out of the window, looking like he was longing to be outside. As before, it was as if there was somewhere else he felt he should be.

Mum tried desperately to make him feel at home,

but over the next few weeks he escaped numerous times, each bid for freedom ending with the police returning him home. Luckily for Mum and Dad, the police were incredibly patient and cheerful about it all. It was always the same two policemen – they must have got to know Blackie very well indeed!

Late one evening in February 1971 Blackie disappeared yet again. Snow had been falling for some time, snowdrifts had blocked most roads and the power was down, so it was dark and very cold. Mum was despondent. Having convinced herself that he didn't like living with us, she was ready to start looking for another family for him. After all, why else would he want to leave a warm loving house for a freezing unwelcoming winter night unless he was unhappy in our home?

A few hours later a familiar police car arrived at the house. 'Come on Blackie,' the tall thin policeman said to him, waving his hand from the car in the direction of Mum's front door. A very wet and cold-looking Blackie, knowing the usual drill by now, slowly got out of the car, walked up to the front door, looked balefully at my mum, then went past her into the living room and lay down, shivering, by the fire.

Mum was now determined to get to the bottom of Blackie's strange behaviour. She'd never thought to ask any questions about Blackie's previous owners, having just assumed they didn't want him any more, like the many other people who left their dogs to roam the streets. But feeling that perhaps there was a chance the police officers might be able to persuade Blackie's old owners to take him back she said, 'I think you ought to take this poor dog back to his original owner.' She spoke with a heavy heart. After all, she didn't really want Blackie to go. My mum just wanted to do what was right for him. 'He's not happy here. I've tried everything to make him feel at home, but nothing works.'

'Mrs Hull, I don't think you understand,' one of the policemen replied.

'I understand I can't bear to see him suffer any more,' she said.

'Mrs Hull, do you remember seeing the old rag 'n' bone man? You know, the old guy with the horse and cart? He used to come round here every Thursday and often had a black dog with him.'

'Um, yes. Jake, wasn't it?' she replied.

'Well, you see, he passed away in January of

hypothermia, and the dog was taken into kennels. Only he kept escaping, and when we eventually found him he would be lying on his old master's grave,' the policeman explained. 'This happened at least four times, and the last time we found him we happened to be talking to one of your husband's friends. He explained you were after a dog and so we brought him here to you.'

'So is that where he is when he goes missing?' Mum asked.

'Yes, every time, we find him just lying on Jake's grave.'

'Oh my God, that poor dog. He must be grieving so bad.' Tears filled her eyes.

'Do you still want us to take him? He can go back to the kennels if you like,' the officer said.

'No, no, he will be safe here.' She smiled, and the officers left.

That evening Mum sat in front of the open fire for hours with Blackie. Gently stroking his head, she told him it was OK to miss his master, and that she would love him and take care of him for ever more.

Talking about this with my mum a few years after I started my career as a professional pet psychic, she explained to me that she had shared communication on a telepathic level she didn't even know was possible until that night. Speaking with Blackie seemed natural to her. Though no words were spoken, there was a bond, an understanding between their two hearts that created a feeling of pure love, the like of which she had never experienced before. Mum said that from the look of acceptance and love in his beautiful dark eyes she knew he could understand everything she was saying, and that night a deep and special bond was built between the two of them. Blackie never strayed again.

Over the months he became so loyal to my mum that they were inseparable. Everyone in the neighbourhood soon knew how much Blackie loved her. If my mum went out, leaving him behind, Blackie would crawl under our garden fence and go looking for her. He would go into every neighbour's house, opening the door with his teeth, walk in and have a look around, desperate to track her down. If the family were there they'd take one look at Blackie and say, 'Jean's not here, Blackie', and with that he'd go to the next house, and so on.

The last house in the long terrace belonged to a little old lady called Doris. If Blackie entered and Mum wasn't there, Doris would guess (usually correctly) that Mum was getting some shopping in for the family. All she needed to say was, 'Jean's at the shops, Blackie', and off he'd bound, looking for all the world as if he couldn't bear to be parted from her for a second longer.

He was such a friendly dog that everyone in the neighbourhood loved him, and they'd always take the time to give him a pat and a smile when they saw him. But, though he was a real character, he could be a bit of a nuisance sometimes too. Not everyone took kindly to his habit of opening doors. Once he opened a neighbour's door when their bitch was on heat and let in about twenty local dogs. Luckily the owner was at hand and called the police to help deal with the milling mass of excited dogs that had suddenly invaded the kitchen. Though at least she was kind enough to tell my mum so that she could come and collect Blackie before he was impounded by the local dog warden.

After this incident an optimistic Blackie returned to the house every day and sat outside the door waiting to be let in so he could see the bitch on heat. The lady who lived there seemed to have learnt her lesson and kept a careful watch, but one day she left her back door open for a breath of fresh air – except air wasn't the only thing she let in. Along with the breeze hurtled a blur of black fur. The two dogs seemed so happy to see each other that the owner said with a sigh, 'Oh, go on then, bloody get on with it!', and she went upstairs to read a book, leaving the two lovebirds to their own devices. Blackie was soon the proud father of six identical puppies.

On 12 May 1971, Mum was in labour for seven hours giving birth to me, and Blackie sat outside the bedroom door for every second. At approximately 6pm the midwife finally announced the arrival of a baby girl. She opened the door to let in my two elder sisters and brother, only to be nearly knocked over by Blackie, who ran straight to my mum and, to the midwife's horror, stuck his wet, shiny nose onto mine. With a big red tongue, he gave me the biggest kiss ever – my kiss by an angel! And he truly was an angel. He never left my side, protecting me and watching over me until the day he passed. Dear old Blackie, we loved you so.

I do believe it was here that my love for the animals

began. Blackie showed our family the true meaning of love – being a loyal companion, protector and best friend. Although my mum doesn't have the clear understanding that I have now about communicating with animals, she achieved a telepathic connection with Blackie that she hasn't experienced before or since. This very special dog touched the hearts of so many people and though he has long since passed to spirit, he watches over us as a guardian angel and is still in our hearts today.

When I was around eighteen months old, my mum, dad, Janice and Julie my two sisters, Richard my brother, myself and Blackie all moved from our home in Kent, where I had been born, up to the Midlands to be nearer my mum's sister Irene. Dad had a new job as a sign installer, putting up signs over cinemas and theatres across the country. Though he was happy to leave his painting and decorating days behind him, the new job meant a great deal of travelling away from home. So my parents agreed on the move and a new start, a new life. Because, more than anything, my mum needed the support of her sister; it couldn't have been easy bringing up four children virtually on her own.

Looking back today at old photos of my mother, I can't imagine Dad ever wanting to spend a single minute away from her. In her day, she was simply stunning: tall, slim, blonde, blue-eyed and fabulously glamorous – think of Doris Day. But jobs were scarce, and the opportunity for travel and decent wages was too good to miss. I should also say that Dad was something of a looker too. I remember later on, when we moved to a new house, one of our neighbours told me she'd seen what looked like a film star walking down the street. As it turned out, it was Dad! He was a real good-looking chap in those days. He was about six foot two, with a handsome, slightly tanned face and jet black hair. He is still very dashing now, even at the age of seventy. Neither my mum nor dad look their age, so I'm hoping the genes pass to me.

We moved into a new three-bedroomed house on a council estate in a town called Bedworth. It's strange what you remember from your early years. I still recall being in my cot at Mavor Drive. My bedroom had my cot and two single beds for my sisters, and on the window was a sticker. I remember it was a thumbs-up

Abbey National sticker! I also had a box swing hanging from our back gate. It was brightly coloured and I loved being lifted into it, to swing away whilst my mum peeled potatoes in a washing-up bowl on the back door step as the sun shone.

Memories of my childhood will stay with me for ever. Bedworth (pronounced Beduff by the locals) was a small town, and I think this helped shape my values even today. The people there were very down-to-earth and decent, and I hope that people think the same of me. We were by no means well off financially, but our family was a strong one. Mum worked hard to bring up her four children (which can't have been an easy task!).

It was at Mavor Drive that my great love of animals began. I spent every moment I could with Blackie our dog. We played fetch with his favourite blue rubber ball for hours and hours, or lay on the grass in the front garden looking up at the clouds. (Well, I was looking at the clouds. He was probably just enjoying the sun and a rare chance of peace and quiet.) I remember squeezing him into my red nylon pushchair, and taking him up and down the street, waving at the neighbours who were looking out of their windows, probably wondering what on earth I was doing. And when the local children stopped and stared I would just smile at them proudly and say, 'Isn't he the most gorgeous baby you've ever seen?'

Luckily for me Blackie went along with all my games, and I think he genuinely enjoyed being pushed about and pampered like a baby; at least he never once tried to escape or showed any indication of unhappiness. In fact, I recall him actually jumping into that pushchair to be pushed around. He was a big dog, and sometimes I wonder how he managed to fit in it.

I adored being around Blackie and any other animal I came across. I suppose this is when I began to realise I was slightly different from other children. I was desperate to be around animals all the time, and I think I was more comfortable with them than I was with the kids I should have been playing with. I remember going to nursery and insisting that Blackie came with me. Mum walked us both to the classroom and then she and Blackie made a quick exit through the classroom door while I was picked up by the teacher, screaming at the top of my voice, waving my arms around and kicking like a mule.

Knowing what was to come, I am sure Mum had

quietly explained to the teacher that dramatic measures would have to be taken to part me from my beloved dog. Very embarrassing to look back on now, but at the time I never wanted to leave Blackie's side. I mean, what on earth would I have in common with twenty other children? I didn't need, or want, to be around them. I just wanted my dog! Perfectly reasonable, wasn't it?

I never did like school much. I was more than capable of learning my lessons, but I had absolutely no interest in anything other than learning about animals and being with them. Instead of the usual pictures of their family, friends and houses that the other children drew, I covered the page with pictures of animals. The others might bring books such as *Charlie and the Train*, or *A Day in the Park* home from school. Not me . . . my first schoolbook was *Pip the Dog*. Unless another child displayed an interest in animals, I didn't really want to mix with them. This meant I only had a handful of like-minded kids to play with. When we played, we tended to sit on our lawn with the hamster I had at the time, or play horses up and down the street, with skipping ropes tied around our waists, neighing continually for all the neighbours to hear.

By the time I was four my parents had saved up enough to buy a house of their own and we moved to a red brick end terrace on another street in Bedworth – Smorrall Lane. It had two large bedrooms and a third smaller room that Richard slept in. Janice and Julie shared a room and Mum and Dad slept with me in the largest of the three. How they ever managed to have a sex life with me in there, I will never know – and perhaps don't want to. Yuk!

The stairs and landing in that house creaked in an unsettling way; the decor was a little fussy by today's standards, and it was rather dark. In fact, everything about it was a bit spooky. The house always seemed chilly and we had no central heating, just a couple of gas fires. On winter mornings it was so cold you could actually see your breath as you tiptoed down the creaky stairs to the outside loo.

The upstairs always seemed most frightening to me. I felt as if I was being watched by a ghostly presence, or a strange entity, something not of this world. I wasn't too sure what it was, but it never failed to give me the creeps, especially when I was alone – something I always tried to avoid. I recall having to get my pencil case from my room and running as fast as I could up the stairs and onto the landing, flying through the door and grabbing it, then racing back down to where I felt safe. I was so fast I would have made Linford Christie look flat-footed.

This happened increasingly regularly and Mum soon got fed up with the thunder of my feet above her. 'Stop banging, Joanne. Slow down,' she would yell up to me, but before she could finish her sentence I would be back beside her, panting and puffing after my sprint for whichever item I'd had to venture upstairs to fetch. Because of this I spent as much time as I could downstairs. The feeling there was so different. It felt jolly, full of fun and a nice place to be.

The ground floor was narrow and long, with a goodsized living room at the front. This was the family room where my mum, sisters and brother spent most of their time, dancing and singing to the many records my dad owned. In fact, he had so many that they took up one whole wall from top to bottom. The other walls were decorated in large brown flowered wallpaper and there was a portrait print of a rather dark and mysterious Spanish lady hanging by the front porch door. My mum loved this picture. The lady had long dark hair swept to one side over her bare tanned shoulder. Her eyes followed you around the room and used to really freak me out. The middle room was our dining room, where we would eat as a family – well, extended family, since my parents operated an open house for all our friends. Mum was fabulous, making everyone welcome, and Dad was just happy to have his family around him. We didn't have much, but Mum and Dad showed love and hospitality to all. The kitchen was tiny. However, my mum managed quite remarkably despite this, cooking dinners and baking cakes for everyone.

Although Mum and Dad were married for twenty-three years, one thing they never really discussed was the psychic world. I suppose Mum grew up knowing more than most as a result of her upbringing by her grandparents. Her Grandma and Grandad Gregg were true spiritualists, having been regulars at their spiritualist church for as long as Mum can remember. My mother's family came from a poor background in Sacriston, County Durham. My nan had been left a widow after her husband was killed in the war. With no real of income to speak of she couldn't afford to bring up her children on her own, so my mum, her brother and her sister were sent to live with relatives.

My mum went to live with one set of grandparents and her siblings went to the other. My nan then went to live and work in a pub as a means of making some kind of living, seeing her children as and when she could.

My mum had a good relationship with her grandparents and grew up happily – she was the apple of their eye. Mum was always taken to the church with them. Her memories of this are quite vague: she remembers going, but not what happened within the church. Unsurprisingly for someone who had been attending the spiritualist church since she was young, she saw nothing unusual in the kinds of things its worshippers discussed. When Mum was about five years old, Grandma Gregg passed to spirit, leaving Grandad Gregg on his own. He would regularly say to Mum that he was off to talk to Grandma in private. And so he would take his pipe and head to the nearby gitty (a type of alleyway) and spend an hour just chatting with her spirit. Neither Mum nor anyone else knew if he was actually speaking with his dead wife, but it seemed to ease the grief Grandad was feeling. All this meant that Mum grew up with the belief that life did exist after death.

My mum's first real psychic experience came soon after my sister Janice was born. It was 1961 and Janice, who was probably only a couple of months old, had just been settled down in her cot at the end of Mum and Dad's bed. Mum was sitting on the bed when all of a sudden she felt a presence; she looked up to see the figure of a man standing over Janice. She recalls feeling totally frozen, not with shock but with amazement as she saw Janice giggle and stare straight at the figure in front of her. The man was dressed in a familiar black overcoat and hat, and Mum remembers recognising him immediately – it was her grandad who had passed to spirit many years before. He stayed for what seemed like a lifetime, smiling down at Janice, though in truth it was probably only a few seconds, and then disappeared into thin air. Obviously Mum was shaken, and even to this day the memory of that extraordinary experience is as fresh as if it had only just happened. Having witnessed an apparition at first hand her belief in life after death was confirmed once and for all.

Later on, Mum would often talk to us about her spiritual experiences. We used to find them spooky but thrilling to hear. I suppose all children love a good ghost story (even if, like me, it scares the living daylights out of them) and in a sense these tales were no different. Talking about spirits and ghostly presences was a normal part of our lives whilst we were growing up. Although I never failed to be terrified by our creaking staircases I was nevertheless fascinated by everything to do with 'the other side'. Even today, Janice and I will happily sit around clutching our cups of tea and nibbling nervously on a bar of Dairy Milk as we swap weird and spooky tales our friends have told us. We just love it – the stories and the Dairy Milk!

After moving in to our house in Smorrall Lane, Mum certainly experienced her share of odd happenings. I particularly remember the day she was pinched on her bottom by a naughty spirit in the kitchen. Since I was the only one at home that day her first thought was that it was me and she turned round to tell me off, only to realise that I was still outside playing. Being the kind of woman she is she just took it in her stride, told the ghost in no uncertain terms where to get off and carried on washing the dishes.

As time went by in that house I gradually began to notice that I was being watched almost constantly by someone or something that was not of this world.

Soon the sense of being observed by a presence I couldn't explain and didn't understand became really uncomfortable. I don't think my fear of going upstairs was unusual: there's nothing strange about a young child being spooked by creaky stairs and dark corridors. However, this was a different experience entirely. Whether it was a ghost, spirit or entity of some other description, it felt a galaxy away from the much more comforting visitations Mum had told us about.

Looking back at the situation now, I'm pretty sure I was unconsciously tuning into something that I'd have run a million miles from if I'd realised what it actually was. This can often happen to young children. Their psychic energies are open and they are known to attract entities and channel poltergeist happenings. There have been many accounts of this through the ages, in church records and stories, documentaries and feature films. For most of us, our openness to the spirit world slowly, naturally closes as we grow older, but there are exceptions. In some cases, for whatever reason, this openness just remains; in others the psychic energy is deliberately reawakened. I think I'm one of those people who have retained the ability I had as a child, though in my case it is actually stronger now.

When I was affected by the presence of this spirit I turned to my animals to keep me safe from my fears. If they were always around me, then I believed nothing could hurt me.

We had various different animals whilst we were in Smorrall Lane. In fact, the house came to resemble a small zoo at times. Although I was still a young girl, people from the neighbourhood had heard how good I was with animals. There were even rumours that I had saved the life of several creatures who'd been on the brink of death. These rumours weren't strictly speaking true, but my reputation as someone who not only loved animals but could heal them too spread nevertheless. Our neighbours often brought me animals that had been found, injured or hurt, and I would take care of them, solve their problems and then give them away to friends. My mum and dad had various discussions at the time to try and limit the number of pets we kept in the house. They were both a bit concerned but I think eventually Mum came to the conclusion that it was better to have me looking after the animals than running wild in the streets. If nothing else, being out in the garden with my pets meant I didn't have to be in the spooky house.

I don't recall Janice, Richard or Julie having any similar experiences; it just seemed to be my mum and myself who were sensitive to the house and its ghosts. I suppose Mum is what you might call a silent psychic, in that she hears, feels and senses the spiritual side of life but has no active connection with it, as much out of choice as anything else. I actually believe that, although she didn't seem to pick up on things in the house as I did when we were young, Janice is almost the same as our mother.

Janice and myself have an uncanny connection. Even though there are ten years between us, we can be at opposite ends of the country when we will sense something at the exact same time. Our psychic connection is pretty special and something only we can understand.

When I was around eight or nine years of age, my dad used to take me horse riding at the local stables every Sunday. I adored being around the horses, and looked forward to my weekly ride on Billy, a white pony who went on to occupy a very special place in my heart. Janice was going out with a boy from college at the time and as it was a sunny day they decided to go for a ride on his motorbike, but Julie came along to the stables with me and Dad. I wasn't too happy about this as we clashed a lot when we were children. I guess you could put it down to sibling rivalry. Moreover, I felt Sundays were for myself and my dad to spend time alone together. Even at such a young age I appreciated how various were the demands on his time. He was a busy dad and sharing the few free hours that were left to him among four children was no easy task. So I knew our time together was precious and resented seeing him split his attention.

Julie was put on top of a pony named Maisie, who was very pretty with a multi-coloured mane and tail and a soft cream coat. For some reason Billy the pony couldn't be ridden that day and so another was chosen for me. I do not recall which pony I was given, but I do remember being most upset at not being able to ride Billy. My communication with Billy was based on a deep emotional loving bond. We were happy to be in each other's company: he would whinny excitedly upon my arrival at the stables, and in return I would wrap my arms around him and give him the biggest cuddle I could muster. He trusted me and I him. We had such a strong mutual understanding. Billy was pleased to do anything I asked of him: walk, trot, canter, or leap over a small show jump with ease. But with other children, he could be stubborn as a mule, sometimes refusing to do anything other than walk. Or he might stand with his head down, sulking, leaving them begging him to move on and flapping their little legs against his flanks. Nothing would make him budge, but he was never like that with me. When I rode him he was fun, exciting and generous – and I loved him.

Just as Dad, Julie and myself were returning to the stables after our hour-long hack, I had a strange sense (one that I'd recognise now as being psychic) that all was not well. I felt something bad was about to happen and an overwhelming feeling of uneasiness flowed through my body. My palms began to get hot, my lips dried out and my tummy churned with fear. The pony beneath me started to tense up, and I could feel every muscle in his body tighten like a coiled spring. Though time seemed almost to stop, in reality events unfolded far too quickly for me to say anything to my dad.

All of a sudden the pony I was riding shot through the entrance to the stables and took off like lightning. I was in total shock as he headed flat out in a gallop towards the stable block, showing no sign of slowing down. All my dad could do was look on helplessly in horror as I tried to bring the pony to a halt. I pulled and pulled on the reins with all my might but my efforts were to no avail. The pony had locked his jaw tight and there was no stopping him. His feet were like thunder under me, the wind was rushing past my face and the large farm gate was drawing closer and closer. I held my breath in fear and braced myself for impact. With a quick twist of his body, the pony avoided the gate by quickly heading left, but this swift movement only served to propel me from the saddle at high speed in the other direction and I ended up flying head first into the gate.

I don't really remember much after the incident, apart from everyone rushing around crying for someone to get help and my dad cradling me in his arms in total shock. The poor man must have feared the worst as my riding hat was completely smashed in on one side.

The ambulance arrived at the stables and I was taken off to our nearest hospital in Nuneaton. At that very moment, my mum, oblivious of my accident, was rushing over to a Coventry hospital where Janice and her boyfriend had been taken after they had an accident on the bike at exactly the same time as mine.

Luckily for Janice and me, we both came out of hospital a few days later having suffered just a few cuts and bruises. And to this day, when things happen to me you can almost guarantee the same will happen to Janice. It's very strange, but it can actually be fun at times. If nothing else we haven't experienced any more simultaneous brushes with death!

Chapter Two

Many of my days as a child were spent watching, drawing or playing horses. To me they were creatures imbued with a mystical energy and I felt empowered just being around them. I felt more at home on top of a horse than I did walking. And I lived from week to week just counting the days until I could ride Billy again. My bedroom was covered wall to ceiling in horse and pony pictures and my scrapbook was full almost to bursting with drawings and diagrams of bridles, saddles and all the other riding equipment I was teaching myself about.

I still didn't enjoy school. As far as I was concerned, school work was for school work's sake. I knew it was important, but all I wanted was to learn about the animals in my life and not boring maths! In retrospect I was silly really, because I was a pretty bright child, and if I had had the will to work I could have done really well at school. However, animals were much more important to me than any lesson could ever be and no amount of moaning from my teachers and parents could change my opinion. More seriously, I was beginning to feel increasingly conscious of not having many friends; I was like a round peg in a square hole, and knowing that high school was looming just served to make me even more worried.

It was clear to the other children at my school that I was slightly different from them. When they played out on their bikes, I just wanted to play with the animals. This hadn't seemed to matter before, but as we grew older so the pressure to fit in and be like all the other girls increased. Inevitably, things came to a head, though it all happened in a strange way. I had been playing with a girl with whom I'd thought I was good friends when, without warning, she turned on me. It was over something really stupid, and I'll never know her reasons for her sudden change of attitude. I think it wounded me all the more because I've never been able to explain it. She was the natural leader of our group of friends so the others just followed her. She gave me a nasty, spiteful nickname which the other girls picked up on too, leaving me feeling hurt and alone.

I was bullied from the moment of entering the school gates in the morning to walking home at the end of the day. I would hear the other children calling me names, and I felt as if my world was falling apart. There was nothing I could do to stop this girl and her friends bullying me. It soon became apparent to my family: I started faking being ill, pretending to have tummy aches, headaches and other such conditions just so I wouldn't have to go to school. Eventually it got so bad that I became a girl trapped at home, refusing to go out and spending every hour with my animals, who felt like my only friends.

My parents and teachers became increasingly desperate as they tried to work out how to solve a crisis that was becoming more serious day by day. My mum had more meetings with the head of the school than I could ever have imagined, and she fought my corner until eventually it was determined that I should move schools after the Easter break. I was relieved and scared at the same time, but excited to start afresh.

My parents decided that it would be a good idea to allow me to make some new friends and become a little more independent before I moved schools. I think my family understood that for me the animals were everything, and so at the young age of just ten, my mum and dad gave me the best early birthday present ever. They booked me on a children-only holiday that involved caring for, riding and learning all about ponies. My mum and dad could not have picked a more perfect present than this, and as we didn't have much money at the time they must have saved every last penny to enable me to attend.

I think my parents were worried I wouldn't want to go as I was so quiet and withdrawn at this point, but for me it was the holiday of a lifetime. I would be safe, I would be with like-minded girls my own age, and best of all I would be with ponies for a whole week. I couldn't believe it.

I felt on top of the world as I packed my little suitcase with all my riding gear, forgetting totally about any daytime clothes. Luckily Mum was on hand to pack extra pants, vests and money – items I felt I wouldn't need. My dad drove me two hours away to the holiday and there was not a tear in sight from me as I said my goodbyes and waved him off, with my battered old brown suitcase at my side. It was covered in the stickers that Richard my brother was collecting, with just a few of horse's heads, puppies and kittens that I had managed to buy with my pocket money of fifty pence a week. These were stuck to the side of the suitcase as if I had claimed my own area. I felt no sadness, for me it was excitement all the way. Something that only increased when I arrived. The first thing I noticed was the smell of horse manure that wafted around the yard is something I breathe in with delight even to this day (I know . . . weird).

The friendly yard manager, whose name was Jenny, took me into her office to sign in. From where we were standing I could see clearly through the office door into the accommodation block. It was like a grey dormitory, with a row of seven neatly made beds along each of the side walls. There was a glass window at one end so the children could see through into a stable. Later on I found out that this was where they would put any mares who were foaling, so the children could watch this amazing event without disturbing the mare. Unfortunately myself and the thirteen other children who were staying that week never did see a mare giving birth, but we heard lots of stories about past births, with all the gory details that children love.

'Don't be afraid to ask lots of questions, Joanne. We

want you to feel at home here, so enjoy your stay and if you need anything, anything at all, you only have to ask,' Jenny said kindly. Then she asked, 'So what experience in horse riding have you had, Joanne?', whilst writing notes on a sheet of paper in front of her. 'Oh, lots,' I replied. 'I ride ponies all the time.'

In truth I maybe only rode for one hour every Sunday, and although I was quite capable, I was by no means a good rider. But I wasn't about to let that stop me now.

And before I could speak another word the quiet yard suddenly became a hubbub of noise and neighing. It was full of horses, about twenty of them, ranging from little Shetlands the size of dogs to horses that seemed as big as a house (well, I was only small).

'We are getting ready for the daily commute back to the fields,' Jenny said. 'Why don't you go out and meet the horses?' She came out after me and handed a sheet of paper to a lady with long dark hair tied neatly into a ponytail. 'OK, Joanne. You can jump on Prancer,' the head groom shouted at me. I stared up at the horse she was pointing to and took a huge gulp. I was in no doubt he was a stunning horse – a deep mahogany brown with a striking jet black mane and tail – but none of the horses had saddles and were sporting only a bridle, and what about his name Prancer? It certainly suited him, as he was dancing around all over the place.

I was not going to let on I was scared, and I certainly wasn't going to tell them I didn't have the experience I had claimed. No one was going to stop me. With a determined look on my face I took hold of the reins and swung myself up onto Prancer. I could feel myself shaking as I balanced my bottom on his back. He was becoming more and more excited as the other children and adults all settled themselves on their chosen mounts. 'Off we go,' shouted the lady up front and, with a leap of faith from myself and a huge leap of excitement from Prancer, we set off up the main road, bareback.

It would be pretty much unheard of today for children to ride school horses along the roads without saddles or hats, but when I was a child it was an everyday occurrence. The stables where I rode every Sunday also did this, and it was the treat of the day if you were chosen to ride one of the ponies bareback to the field. Quite amazing by today's standards, and very dangerous.

To say my heart was in my mouth as I struggled to control the horse beneath me would be an understatement. Cars were flying past, but the other riders were laughing and joking with each other, paying no attention to my situation. There was nothing for it but to talk to the horse, to try and calm him down, so I began chatting quietly to him. 'Slow, Prancer, slow. I'm not very good. Please help me.' I leaned closer towards his ears and whispered again. 'Please slow down. Stay quiet. Please,' I begged him, and within a second he was walking at ease, relaxed and happy.

The lady behind called up to me, 'Hey kid, what you done to that damn horse? Ain't never seen him so quiet!' I couldn't even turn my head to answer her, but just yelled back, 'Um, don't know. I suppose he is just looking after me,' whilst giving Prancer a shaky pat on his neck for doing just that – it was a thrill to see he'd understood me.

We had been riding for about ten minutes when I heard a commotion at the front of the line. The girls were calling out something to us at the back. For a few seconds I couldn't work out what they were saying, but then the lady in front of me turned her head and gave me a look of horror. I heard the words, 'Look out! Tractor coming! Whoever's on Prancer needs to be extra careful.'

Oh my God, I was riding Prancer!

'Keep him steady,' another shouted. 'He hates them!'

But before anyone could come to my aid, Prancer had spotted the tractor coming towards him. I felt him shake all over, trembling with fear. Then, in a split second, only two hooves were on the ground, and the other two were high up in front of me. I held on for dear life.

'Somebody help her,' shrieked the lady in front of me.

But it was strange. I whispered to Prancer as the tractor approached us, 'It's OK. I will look after you as you have me. We will be safe together. Come down now, Prancer. Feel safe. I will look after you.' With my soft words, all four hooves were back on the ground and we were trotting calmly past the tractor.

'Well ridden!' the head groom shouted, but I felt that I didn't ride at all. I just held on and helped the horse to stay calm, and he trusted my words.

For the next week people would not stop talking about how bravely and calmly Prancer and I had passed the tractor. And that it was the first time anyone had managed to do that with him. One of the grooms later told me that in Prancer's previous home he had been run over by a tractor as a young horse and that was why he had such a fear of them. No one could quite believe his change. But my connection with Prancer was clear for all to see and I was in no doubt that day that Prancer could hear my words.

Although I wasn't truly aware of my psychic connection with animals at this time, I took it for granted that they could hear me. After all, whenever I asked an animal to behave in a certain way, it usually happened. At first I had assumed that everyone else could speak with the animals too, but now I was becoming more conscious that my ability to communicate with them was unusual, and perhaps a little strange.

I adored the week I spent at the yard. Looking back, we were pretty much left to our own devices once the formal teaching was done. It could never happen in this day and age, when children are so mollycoddled they can hardly breathe. But back then everything was quite relaxed and easy-going, and you could just do what you wanted so long as you stayed in the confines of the yard. The staff were friendly but it was being around other children like me that made it so special. I can't remember any child in particular as we all got on so well. It was a perfect holiday, with everyone helping each other and enjoying each other's company.

We sat and chatted for hours on end about the day's adventures on horseback, treating the ponies as if they were our own. Well, they were, at least for that week. It was just magical – a whole week living and breathing horses.

From time to time I went to stay with my auntie Irene for the weekend. Irene is my mum's sister, tall, with auburn hair, and a really lovely person to be around. She used to cook bacon sandwiches with lots of extra fried onions as a treat.

I loved staying at their house, but I missed being around the animals. Caroline (my cousin who is a few years younger than me) didn't really have pets, apart from a blue budgie called Joe that wouldn't sit still for a second, and repeated his name over and over, driving everyone mad. And so I would play outside in the garden, catching butterflies and recording the different colours in my scrapbook, whilst Caroline played indoors with dolls and colouring books.

Even though we had different interests, we always managed to have a great time. Caroline was a quiet, very feminine girl with bright red hair and freckles. One Saturday morning, at around ten, Caroline and I were playing in the front garden when I heard a strange noise coming from a neighbouring garden. It was unlike anything I had ever heard before.

'Can you hear that?' I asked Caroline.

'What?' she replied.

'Shhh. Listen,' I whispered.

She turned and looked at me as if I was mad. She could hear nothing.

I could hear a tiny voice calling for help, but it wasn't a human voice. Imagine a small creature crying out for help, but instead of the usual noise an animal might make, it was as though words were fitting to the noise in exact sequence. I felt panic, and my heart began to race.

I knew I was connecting with something, because I felt different, and my heart was beating faster, just as it used to on the landing in our spooky home. I was becoming more sensitive to sounds around me, but at the same time my focus was feeling drawn to the cries for help.

I could tell Caroline wasn't feeling the same connection. She looked confused and a little apprehensive about what was coming next as I walked purpose-fully across the lawn and out of the garden, towards the noise, with Caroline running behind.

About four houses down I stopped dead in my tracks. I looked down at the small wooden fence in front of me, and to my horror saw a little sparrow hanging upside down by its legs, screaming with fear and flapping its wings violently. Somebody had tied each leg with string and then attached it to the fence. All I could hear were tiny screams of 'Help me, help me'. I could hear her words, I could feel her panic, I could sense her fear.

Caroline was terrified – of what, I do not know – but I knew instinctively exactly what to do. I shouted at her to go and get some scissors, and I'd never seen her run that fast before. I'm not sure if it was the desire to help the bird or my tone of voice. I suspect it to be the latter. Within seconds she was back, handing me a pair of scissors. I gently cut the string from the fence and removed it from the sparrow's legs.

I held the little bird in the palms of my hands as we walked slowly back to the house. Sitting outside on the grass, I explained to Caroline in a matter of fact way that I needed to calm it down, and proceeded to tell the bird she would be safe and free. Looking back,

I was using the natural psychic ability that I use today, something we all have. However, as a child my ability was still developing. Knowing what to do would just come to me, and was now saving the life of an animal.

Calming animals down and understanding their needs, explaining their fears to people and helping to overcome problems were all becoming as easy as breathing to me. So many times during my childhood the animals had helped me through hard times, lonely times and sad times and now it was my turn to help them. And although I wasn't yet fluent with this ability and didn't fully understand it, I felt more and more comfortable with it. The idea of there being a real meaning to my life felt amazing. I was determined always to help any animal that needed me.

Poor Caroline was shocked at the sight of me even touching the sparrow, though I can never understand why anyone wouldn't want to. Birds are soft, warm and just beautiful to hold. At first the bird was shaking slightly, and I could feel her heartbeat as she sat neatly in my cupped palms. Not once did she try and fly from my hands. She felt safe in my care, and I too began to calm down. My senses were still fully alert to the bird, but first my arms and then my hands began to relax.

I felt a soft tingle run through my hands to the tips of my fingers. The bird's little heart, which had been pumping so hard, soon started to calm and slow down.

'OK, you are safe now. If you want to fly, go ahead. You are safe,' I whispered to her. Caroline jumped up in fear and stood well back in case the bird flew too close to her. I opened my palms to the sky and willed the little bird to fly.

I felt warm and fuzzy inside and very pleased with myself for rescuing the sparrow. I never even gave the sparrow calling out a second thought, and perhaps at that time I thought it was perfectly normal. To me a bird is every bit as beautiful as the dog or cat or even horse b⁄ my side. I wondered why Caroline couldn't hear the sparrow. Perhaps her cry was meant only for my ears. Was this gift just for me? Could I really communicate with animals in a way that was different from other people?

I had a few good friends when I was growing up in Smorrall Lane. One of these was Marcia, a very pretty, rosy-cheeked girl full of fun and laughter.

I envied Marcia and her family. They lived in a large Victorian home, nothing like our small terraced house. It had a large open fireplace with polished horse brasses down each side. The house was so full of fun, very much as my own was, but in a more *Little House on the Prairie* type of way. There were three girls, their mum, dad and grandma. Whereas in our house it was not only us kids, but our friends as well, I never saw anyone else at Marcia's house, just the family and myself. They were always so happy and perfect.

On Sundays, the girls always had to wear what their mum called their 'Sunday best'. The dresses were so lovely, all frills and flowers. At my house we wore anything that my mum had time to wash – she managed two jobs and a family of four, so 'Sunday best' was the last thing on her mind. I remember on a number of occasions pretending I too was wearing my 'Sunday best'. I would put on a party dress from my wardrobe and parade around like a princess. The dresses always had crayon marks or ink stains down them due to my artistic drawings of horses and dogs, which I still do even to this day.

Marcia and myself used to play for hours and hours

in the garden, building rockeries and planting weeds. We would lie on the lawn and make animals out of the clouds, a game I used to play with Blackie when I was young. Best of all was playing horses. This involved a skipping rope, lots of neighing and an imagination anyone would be proud of. I used to skip about with the skipping rope reins round my waist, whinnying for all to hear, with Marcia running behind me, trying desperately to hang on to this wild pony with all her might! It was simple back then: ponies were my passion. My bedroom walls were covered from head to toe in pony pictures, and my every moment was spent either drawing ponies or reading about them. I was, as I used to tell my penpals, one hundred per cent pony mad.

On this particular day Marcia and I were playing the usual games when I felt someone or something watching us. I stopped what I was doing and turned around, and there, staring back at me, were the most beautiful dark brown eyes. My breath was taken away at the beauty of this animal. He was tall and graceful, and had the most gorgeous long nose I had ever seen. He was a deep mahogany-coloured greyhound.

'Look, Marcia,' I whispered.

She turned to look at him and, like me, fell instantly in love with the hound that stood before us.

He walked over and nudged his muzzle softly against my hand, and then against Marcia's, wagging his long tail. 'It was the nudge of friendship,' we used to say. The three of us became friends straightaway. I remember wondering why such an amazing dog would be homeless. Where had he come from? Was he on a journey? And could I ask him, talk with him perhaps? At this stage in my life I was still a little unsure if my ability was real even though it had seemed to have such a wonderful effect on the sparrow and the horse Prancer. Looking back now, I can't understand why I didn't just ask him. What did I have to lose?

One thing was for sure – he was hungry and needed some TLC, so we took him back to Marcia's and gave him a good meal. Marcia's dad agreed to let him stay in one of the outbuildings which was warm and dry.

Over the next two weeks the greyhound never left our side. He followed wherever we went, grateful for the love and attention we gave him. We advertised for his owners through home-made posters drawn in black and red felt tip pen, but to no avail. Then early one morning Marcia's dad found me cuddling the dog with tears in my eyes.

'What's wrong?' he asked, looking down at me.

'I'm saying goodbye,' I replied. I explained that my mum had decided to take the family for a week's holiday, and that it would mean leaving the dog.

'But he'll be here when you get back,' Marcia's dad told me.

As I looked into the dog's eyes earlier that day, I heard an inner voice. It was his, I was sure of it, soft and warm. It wasn't mine and no one else was speaking at the time.

'Goodbye,' the voice said softly.

I felt a bolt of pure emotion shoot directly into my heart, and the words that seemed to form in my head from my own consciousness made me gasp with breathlessness. The tears trickled down my cheeks as I began to get that familiar feeling of warmth. My heartbeat speeded up and all my focus was directed on the animal. As my senses came alive I could almost hear the sound of his heartbeat.

I gazed into the greyhound's dark eyes and with acceptance I uttered the word right back to him: 'Goodbye.' I held him tight in my arms and prayed he would be safe. I had a strong feeling deep in the pit of my tummy that this was the last time I would ever see him. The greyhound looked back at me, and I could see by the slight softening of his eyes that he had understood me. Wiping my tears away with my hand, I gave him the biggest kiss on his beautiful long nose. And I felt the unconditional love he gave so freely.

That was the last time I saw him. Whilst I was away on holiday the dog vanished. Marcia was so upset. She looked everywhere for him, but he had gone, and was never seen again. Maybe his journey hadn't finished, or maybe he found his way home. We will never know. I just hoped he was safe.

Looking back to this experience it's interesting to see the same pattern of communication appearing over and over: the feeling of warmth, unconditional love and a speeding heartbeat, the senses awakening to a higher frequency and the focus being directed at the animal in question, almost blocking out any background interference. It would prove to be my typical method of communication by connection, something that would stay with me for life.

By now I was really becoming aware that I was slightly different from other children and I couldn't understand why others didn't feel the empathy for animals that I did. I had gradually collected various species of furry creatures, who lived quite happily in our back garden in different-sized sheds and runs. One day, I received a gift of two tiny cream-coloured mice. They were so cute, with their little rounded ears, inquisitive faces and whiskers that twitched in the summer air. I thought they were adorable. One was called Minnie, the other Mickey, and I was so excited about having my new companions come to live with me.

I found an old hamster cage in the shed at the top of our garden and began to clean it out with soap and water so they would have a lovely place to live. I put some sawdust, food and water into the cage and introduced the two little mice to their new home. They immediately began scurrying about, investigating their new surroundings. They looked so happy, but I felt they shouldn't be locked in. Who was I to cage these little mice up? So I sat in front of them and explained how I would give them their freedom: they could eat and sleep in the cage, but be free to come and go as they pleased.

Leaving the cage open in the shed, I wandered back down the garden to the house, where my parents knew nothing about the mice in the shed. Of course they were fully aware I had lots of different animals in the garden, but they usually left me to it. Most of the animals would come and go, for one reason or another. Some were rescued and re-homed whilst others were only with me whilst friends went on their holidays.

The next morning I raced up to the shed, heart thumping, wondering if the mice were there. I opened the door to see an empty cage in front of me. I was gutted! They were nowhere to be seen. I sat on an empty box and called out in the hope they would hear me. 'Minnie, Mickey, please come home.' My pleas didn't go unheard, and out of the corner of my eye I saw two little cream-coloured mice come scurrying across the workbench and up into their cage. I was amazed, and I remember thinking what clever mice they were, using their home like a hotel.

So this was the start of their little adventure. I would spend hours in the shed just chatting away with them, then wave them off as they scuttled along the work-bench, down some plastic piping onto the floor and out through the back of the shed into the fields beyond. What they did out in those fields I have no idea, but I knew they were happy because the feeling of happi-ness they shared with me was undeniable. I knew my connection with the mice was more than the usual child-to-pet connection: I was able to communicate on a deeper level. It was astonishing to me. My ability seemed to be getting stronger by the day; it seemed I was good at communication, and the animals were proving over and over that it was real.

Being around these mice and feeling their magic was one of those mini light-bulb moments in my life. The details of my communication process with animals were becoming clearer. I was learning to trust my gut feeling, and almost expecting a connection to happen.

My dad had been working away from home when I got the mice, and when he returned he didn't go near the shed for months. Then one day I heard the loudest scream ever and saw my dad running down the garden path at great speed. Now, I think it was hilarious, but it could have given my dad a heart attack. He's terrified of mice! It turned out that he had gone into the shed to fetch a gardening tool, only to be greeted by a sea of multi-coloured mice. According to him there were hundreds, but that's a slight exaggeration I expect. Either way, Minnie and Mickey had been having a grand time, mating with the wild mice from the field and using their home like a hotel party pad, inviting all their friends, relatives and numerous children back. Needless to say I had strict instructions to house them in a new secure home, where house rules were firmly enforced.

As for the rest of the mice, I sat down and asked them, 'Please mice, only appear when my dad is not around, as he is scared of you.' It worked. They heard my request loud and clear and only ever came into the shed when I was around. And I have to say, what a sight they all were. Minnie and Mickey must have been very busy!

Chapter Three

The years were slowly passing and school was becoming more and more tedious for me. I never enjoyed it. Well, I say never, but I enjoyed English literature and language, probably because I could write or read about animals for my essays. And in history lessons I could write and research about heroic animals, so all these subjects made total sense to me. As for biology, oh, that was my worst nightmare! I remember the day we had to dissect a frog. Our teacher, Mr Redburn, hooked out the pickled frog bodies from a large glass jar and handed them out to the class as the pupils cheered and jumped with excitement. I ran out of the room in tears. I just couldn't do it. All I could see was people torturing those poor animals – and the usual boys in the corner, holding the corpses up and dangling their legs in front of the girls next to them so they would scream. I loved animals, so why would I want to cut them up?

I never wanted to be in school, and it didn't help that

the situation at home was a little under strain. I wasn't sure what was going on, but there was a really odd feeling in the pit of my tummy. I sensed my mum was unhappy and I think I didn't want to ask her about it in case my question made her even more upset. As a family, we rarely argued, and always tried to have a positive outlook on life, but emotions were bubbling away under the surface like a volcano just waiting to erupt.

Then one afternoon my mum called me into the living room and sat me down on the sofa. I don't recall most of what she said to me that day. I don't even recall feeling upset. Maybe pretending things weren't actually happening was my way of coping.

What I do remember is my mum asking me the question she would have been dreading: 'Do you want to live with me or your father after our divorce?'

Divorce? Where did this come from? It was a bolt from the blue. Yes, I knew something was wrong, but never once did I think it was my mum and dad's relationship. When I sit here and think back to this time, the strange thing is I cannot remember ever hearing Mum and Dad argue. I'm sure they did at some point, but I know it certainly wasn't whilst I could hear.

There was no question where I wanted to be. My

life with the animals was at Smorrall Lane, and I knew Dad would always be part of our life, so I don't remember feeling concerned about not seeing him. He was away with his job a lot in those days – more often than not he'd be in London – so really, what would change? Nothing, apart from him not living with us. Within weeks, Dad had moved out into a new house in the local area and life continued as if nothing had happened. If anything, we saw him more now than we did before he and Mum split. And he still took me to my riding lessons every week at our local stables. I accepted the situation for what it was. There were no tears, no drama, just a sense of us all getting on with life as it was now to be.

My dad always worked hard to provide for his family, and in my eyes he has been a wonderful dad. However, perhaps he wasn't such a great husband. He had an eye for the ladies, and from what I can gather he was unfaithful at least twice during my parents' marriage. I think Mum knew, but her priority was always keeping the family together, and she sheltered us children from this information at the time. It couldn't have been easy for her, and even to this day she doesn't like to talk about it.

The truth about Mum and Dad's divorce came out much later, when I was an adult. Mum briefly explained that my dad had been having an affair with a younger lady. Mum decided enough was enough and made the decision that their marriage was at an end, although she still loved him deeply. She seemed so brave to me at the time but she must have been heartbroken. After all, my father was the love of her life, but she had heard he was in love with this woman and knew she couldn't stop him leaving.

The guilt of leaving his children must have been too much for my dad at times and he treated us all on occasions. My treat was something I had only ever dreamed of, but now it was about to become real.

'Joanne, I am taking you to find a pony,' Dad said, smiling at me as I clicked my seat belt in the car. I stared at him in disbelief.

'What do you mean?' I asked.

'Well, I think it's about time you had your own pony, so let's go shopping!' he explained.

My heart felt like it was in my mouth. A pony of my own! I was stuck for words.

We drove around for miles, looking at ponies in fields, with my dad now and then stopping to ask yard owners if they knew of any ponies for sale. In my mind I kept seeing a picture of a bright chestnut, and I explained that was the type I would like if we could find one. After a day of searching and asking about we had found nothing, so Dad promised to take me to a local horse dealer who might be able to help.

I was so excited that I awoke very early the next day, just as the sun was rising. We headed off down to the dealing yard to see the man with the horses. I jumped out of the car and went to the field gate, and there in front of me were about fifteen assorted horses and ponies. A girl's dream! I left my dad to talk money with the dealer as I scanned the herd of horses for the chestnut I had seen in my dream. Coming straight towards me was a very familiar face. His nostrils were grey, his coat thick and bushy and there was a look of happiness to see me written all over his beautiful face.

'Billy!' I yelped. 'Billy, what are you doing here?' Oh no, why is he at the dealer's yard? I asked myself. This pony should be at the riding school. My heart sank, and all my excitement disappeared in a flash. I began to feel a flush of tears as I stroked his soft velvet nose.

'Oh, Billy, I love you so much. You have been a wonderful friend to me, haven't you my lovely boy?' I whispered, tears trickling down my cheeks. The realisation that my white pony Billy, the furry friend who taught me to ride when I was three and faithfully looked after me at every step of my childhood, had been thrown on the scrap heap of life was too much to take in. I was devastated. Billy had been my favourite pony all my life. And now here he was, standing in front of me once again, and I knew that I couldn't or even wouldn't be able to save him. I leant over the fence that separated us and kissed him on the forelock. 'I love you Billy, and always will,' I whispered through the tears.

'Ahhh, you don't want that old goat!' a stout-looking man shouted as he and my dad approached.

I turned and looked at my dad and then at Billy. With a look of desperation I mumbled, 'It's Billy, Dad! It's Billy!'

I saw my dad take a deep breath, but before he could say anything the stout man piped up, 'He's not for sale. He's going tomorrow. Far too old for you, my lovely. Now come and see what I have that's just come in.' And he ushered us through the field, leaving Billy standing watching my every move. My heart felt like it had been ripped out. I was distraught.

'Come on, Joanne,' Dad said, trying to keep the conversation light. 'Realistically he is just too old. There's no point buying him. You want something you can have fun on, don't you?'

'Yes, but . . .'

'Joanne, I know you love Billy, but he isn't young enough, is he?'

I felt my head turning reluctantly from side to side in agreement. I loved Billy with all my heart, and desperately wanted to argue with what they were saying, but the words wouldn't come. The man pointed out a few possibilities for me, all under the age of seven, apparently a perfect age for my requirements. But all I wanted was Billy. He wasn't the pony I needed, but in my heart he was the pony I wanted. The chestnut pony in my dreams had been erased.

I took one last look at Billy as we left the field that day, and whispered in my head that I would always love him. Somewhere deep in my heart I heard him whisper right back. I will never forget Billy. Never.

It was nearly two weeks before my dad took me back to the dealer. Billy had gone and I knew where. At the grand age of twenty-four or so, there was only one place left and it wasn't a retirement home. I know my dad struggled not to buy him; after all, Billy had played a big part in his life too. But he decided to take the advice of the dealer and buy me a much younger pony that was able to do the activities I would be wanting.

Dad stopped at the entrance to the field and pointed to a bright red chestnut pony. 'There, he's yours!' he smiled.

My emotions were all mixed up. Something I had waited for all my life was standing a few yards in front of me, yet part of me could never forgive myself for not fighting harder to save Billy. I wish I had. This has been one of the biggest regrets of my life. Of course my dad's reasons for not taking Billy were right. His daughter needed a pony she could take to the local gymkhana and win rosettes, a pony she could spend long summer days out riding. Billy was too old, too slow and almost at the end of his days. But I still wonder, why didn't I argue, fight for him, beg for him?

The chestnut pony I had seen in my dreams was now all mine. Maybe you can't change the future. Maybe if I was meant to have Billy I would have seen him in my dreams and not the chestnut. Perhaps our fate is mapped out before us. And maybe a small part of my dad's guilt disappeared after buying me a pony. I was certainly eternally grateful, but to be honest I never held my dad or mum accountable for their split, and certainly didn't expect a pony out of such a difficult time for them.

As for my mum and dad, they stayed good friends and Dad has always been around when we needed him. Eventually he married the woman he had fallen in love with, and all his children were by his side. My feelings about the day are mixed: I was pleased Dad was happy, but worried Mum would be sad. So we all made an effort to make Mum feel special, which I am sure she appreciated at the time. And life ticked on.

My intuition around animals was becoming stronger and stronger over the years. I could sense their emotions, feeling their sadness and happiness, and I knew when they needed my help. I knew what they were thinking, and I thought I could hear their words. But I still didn't realise that other people didn't all have the same feelings as me.

I had often heard about psychic mediums from

friends and family, finding the thought of speaking with dead people a very scary concept, and not something I was keen on finding out more about. It never crossed my mind that just as a psychic medium connects to human spirits, so I would later use the same technique to connect with animals. I didn't see the similarity at this time. Yes, I had some sort of intuition, but psychic ability? I never connected the two.

I often walked home from school with my friend Emily, who had a similar interest in animals. She kept an enormous pet rabbit at the bottom of her garden. He had white fur and red eyes, with a body the size of a cocker spaniel. Even to this day I don't think I've seen a rabbit as big. He was a bit of a bully, and used to chase Emily's mum's two Border collies up and down the garden.

It was a four-mile trip to and from school. Halfway home we had to cross a motorway bridge. There was a fence about eight feet high at either end, to stop people getting onto the motorway from the steep embankment. We had crossed the bridge hundreds of times, but on this particular afternoon we stopped and looked down over the railings of the bridge at the traffic below. We were laughing and joking around. Emily started waving at the traffic, and the people waved right back. We giggled and walked on, but just as we reached the end of the bridge I heard a cry for help: not a person's cry for help, but that sense I had before when I heard the sparrow cry. It was an animal, I was sure. Within seconds I began to feel the connection starting – the rapid heartbeat, the feeling of my focus shifting to the cry. I could feel a warmth, but there was also a feeling of desperation and fear. These were all familiar signs to me.

'Emily, there's an animal in trouble,' I whispered, trying to follow the cries.

But Emily was oblivious to the sound, and she suggested that I was hearing things.

I couldn't see any sign of any creature other than ourselves on the bridge. I turned around and to my amazement there it was: a small whimpering noise coming from behind the fence. I stopped suddenly and there I saw the most beautiful dark brown eyes. They were piercing into my heart, begging for my help.

'What's the matter?' Emily asked.

I turned to look at her and pointed in the direction of the noise.

'Look,' I whispered.

'What?' she asked, looking slightly worried.

'Look at him, Emily. Look behind the fence!'

We both stared at the little dog in front of us. He was small, very furry and incredibly cute.

'But what's he doing behind the fence? That's the motorway embankment,' she said.

I listened to try and hear what the dog was saying to us, and I heard the very faint words, 'Help me get under the fence. Help me, please.'

I turned to Emily and said, 'I know what he's trying to tell us. He wants out of there. Quick, Emily. Help me.'

We dropped our school bags and ran over to the little dog, realising very quickly that he had no way of escaping through the strong chain link fence.

'What are we going to do?' Emily asked.

I looked at the little dog and he looked back at me. Then I got it. He spoke the word straight to my mind . . . Dig!

'Dig under the fence, Emily,' I squealed.

'How? We have no spade.'

'We have to use our hands. Just dig,' I insisted.

The little dog gave me an approving look and I knew

he understood. In a flash he began to dig under the fence with his paws.

'Look, Joanne,' Emily said in amazement. 'He's helping us!'

The three of us dug and dug until finally there was enough room for the little dog to squeeze his tummy under the fence and be united with us. It was a joyous moment! We were exhausted and our hands were sore from digging the hard earth, but his tail was wagging wildly and he landed uncontrollable kisses over our faces. He was so very grateful.

He followed us home to my house, sticking to my side like glue.

'Mum,' I shouted, as we arrived.

I saw her face as she looked down at yet another stray animal that I had brought home.

'And who's this?' she asked.

So we told her the story of how we had dug beneath the motorway fence to rescue the little dog. My mum found him a good home as I just could not keep any more animals. I kissed him farewell and cried myself to sleep, but I'm sure he was very happy and loved by his new family. I just thank God we were there to rescue him that day. He could so easily have strayed in front of a car, confused and wondering where his family was. The only way he could have got onto the embankment was by being dumped from a car on the motorway. I never could understand why or how people could do such a thing to such a lovely creature.

By now I was about fourteen years of age and hated school even more than ever. In fact, my attendance records were disgraceful. I wasn't ill – I just wanted to be with my pony as much as I could. I would often skip school with friends to spend the afternoon grooming and playing around with our ponies. At around quarter past three we would head home and pretend we had been in school all day. I was lucky that so many of my friends at high school had ponies. Warwickshire was the home of some of the most fantastic gymkhanas a girl could wish for. I was now able to spend time with like-minded girls of the same age who also wanted to spend time with their ponies and not in education. We had lots in common.

My poor mum was completely unaware of my truancy until the wag man came knocking. He was the school truancy warden and everyone, including the parents, was terrified of him. I got in so much trouble for skiving and did try several times to be a good girl and stay in my classes. My attendance would be good for about four weeks and then I would be unable to concentrate on my work and the truancy would start all over again. I longed for the day I could leave school and work with the animals.

Two years later, I still had a few months to go before I was legally able to leave school and so took a part-time job at a local egg farm. But I was really keen to leave school for good and get a full-time job. Although I was happy at home and my family life was good, I had always felt a need to explore. My parents encouraged me to follow my dreams rather than stay in the same town, and I knew what I wanted to do. I wrote to about eight riding stables around the country, asking for work as a groom. I had looked at a map of the country and thought Kent or Somerset would be nice. Why? Because in my head they sounded sunny. Sunny represents happy, and that's what I am attracted to: sunny, happy places and people. I know it sounds odd now, but that really was the reason.

I hoped and crossed my fingers for a reply from the yards I had written to, praying they would say I had a job. I felt excitement about my future, and was not at all nervous. To my delight I received three responses, all of which offered me a job working with the horses, so now I had a choice to make. I was leaving home for some time and wanted to be sure I made the right move.

I sat with our family dog, who was very clever and used to share secrets with me. I decided he would show me what to do. We had a strong bond and often communicated feelings and emotions. Being with him was always fun. My mum and I had bought this dog from a school friend when he was just eight weeks old. When we went to collect him, he was the only puppy in the litter of ten to come over and lick my face and stay with me, whilst all the other pups ran around the garden with tug toys in their mouths. It was decided he was the one we were taking home. Neither my mum nor myself could think of a name for him, so on the way home on the bus, with the puppy safely snuggled up in my arms, we began looking at the signs and billboards for names that would suit him.

'Andrex?' my mum laughed.

'No. That's a Labrador's name,' I giggled.

'Cola?' I said, as I saw a man drinking a bottle of Coke at the side of the road.

'Metro?' Mum said, seeing a car on a billboard.

We both looked at each other, and although it was an odd name for a dog, somehow it seemed to suit him perfectly. And so Metro it was, with a nickname of Mettie.

With the three work offer letters in front of us I asked him, 'What do you think Mettie? Which one shall I go for?'

I heard the words, 'Follow your instinct,' in my mind. I looked at him and smiled. Was he speaking to me? The voice was mine, but with a twist of a male presence to it, deep and deliberate, wise and precise. Could it just be my subconscious? I wondered which it was, but trusted what I had heard. I had already had some remarkable verbal communications with animals and felt this probably wasn't any different. OK, I had never heard Mettie through voice before, but we had often had non-verbal communication. Wow, how brilliant that he could talk too, I thought to myself.

'Somerset sounds kind of summery, don't you think? But I'm drawn to the people in Kent. It's less money but they seem nice.'

And as a sign of approval Metro took his paw and placed it right on top of the letter from the Kent yard.

'OK,' I laughed. 'I get the message!'

My family was thrilled at my choice of career and supported my decision. My dad even offered to drive me all the way down to my new job on my starting date. It was a big step for a young sixteen-year-old, but I was sure I was making the right move and positive I would be safe around the horses. They had always looked after me in the past and I felt confident the future would be no different.

I said my goodbyes to my friends and family, and to Mettie, reassuring him I'd be home to see him again soon. I wasn't sad to leave home at all. I loved my new job and loved being around the yard owners, Mollie and Steve. They were kind and looked after their stable hands well. Being the baby of the bunch, I needed that security. After all it was my first real job and I had chosen to go miles from home to work with my first love, horses. Mollie was a rosy-cheeked lady, a great cook and a loving but firm mother figure. Steve was jolly, always laughing but always busy, either buying horses, selling horses or delivering horses. I found the whole situation really exciting. What fun we had in those days!

I grew close to a girl called Heidi. I remember her vividly because on her second day at the yard she was out catching some horses when she was trapped between two thoroughbreds who were arguing at the gate over food. The taller of the two went to bite the other but missed and instead bit Heidi's ear. She came running into the kitchen, holding her ear with blood pouring from it. I can't remember if her ear ended up permanently damaged, but it was a pretty bad incident.

We spent our days cleaning out stables, exercising horses and saying goodbye to them. Steve often took two of us to the local horse sales, to ride horses he had in mind to buy. He would be walking quickly to get an early glimpse of the stock for sale that day, and I would look around too; this was where I saw what some people think of these wonderful, intelligent animals.

It was an incredible sight. There were rows and rows of horses, lined up bum to bum with just enough room for us to walk between them. And lots of men, chatting in strong accents, looking unclean and rough, some laughing, some checking horses' teeth by almost putting their dirty hands in their mouths, and others spitting into their filthy palms and shaking hands, obviously sealing a deal.

On the surface the sale was full of life, noise and excitement. It oozed with the glorious smell of horses. However, when I looked closer, I was connecting to each and every one, just as I did with animals when I was younger. Using what I know now to be my psychic ability, I could feel the broken hearts of the animals, the mistrust and misuse. There were young foals, terrified, screaming as loud as they could for their mums, who had obviously been separated far too early. There were horses who were too old for anything and were for sale to the highest meat man bidder on the day. And there were poor horses who had once been loved by their owners and yet had somehow ended up at the sales. The dealers were always really rough with the animals. I suppose they were expecting the worst – biting, kicking and bad behaviour – but most of them were just full of fear.

I remember Steve pointing out how to tell if a horse had been drugged for the sales to hide psychological issues. He said, 'Look, Joanne, if a horse is drugged you can see as the manhood is often relaxed,' and then he laughed uncontrollably at my embarrassment as my face went scarlet. Although he found it funny, he was right. Often a horse's manhood would be hanging down, his eyes would look sleepy, with his head down between his front legs. We were warned about such cases, because the horse's devilish side would appear as the drugs wore off, which could be really dangerous.

I often wondered how they ended up like this. I'm sure they weren't wicked and dangerous as young foals with their mums. What had we humans done to these poor animals? I realised then that a lot of people don't care. They abuse and neglect animals, treating them dreadfully, when in fact they feel everything we do: love, grief, loss, anger, happiness, loneliness, contentment and hurt. Why do some people understand this and others don't? I cannot answer this.

These animals weren't bad, they were angry: angry at people, angry at their circumstances, angry at the world. In my experience, animals are not born bad, but sometimes the only way they can communicate with humans is through violence and anger.

There were four girls working at the yard, me being one of them, and I had moved out of the main house into a little caravan at the side of the stables. It was my way of having some independence. Sharing a room with three other girls was fun, but it was not my idea of being an independent young woman, especially one who had a new boyfriend. He was an up-and-coming talent in the showjumping circuit, and I thought he was fabulous. After all, he loved horses! His name was Will and he was nineteen years old, very tall, with handsome good looks and short black hair. He could ride any horse he was given and would always be in the winning ribbons at shows. We hung out together as much as we could, attending local dances, shows and other events arm in arm. I felt grown up and free for the first time. I remember trying to speak with Will about the animal voices I could hear, but he laughed it off and said I was nuts. And in order not to be ridiculed further I didn't pursue the topic. Will and I were both crazy about horses and crazy about each other, so nothing else seemed to matter.

The little caravan was my oasis, a place I could call my own while still not breaking ties with the rest of the house. I had all my most precious photographs of my family pinned on the wardrobe door, lemon tea by my kettle and Radio Caroline on the transmitter above my bed. It was heaven.

We girls would wake at six thirty every morning and feed our horses, giving them water and putting fresh hay in the stalls. Once done, we would go into the main house to be greeted by Mollie and her fresh hot toast, real butter and a banquet of different jams, honey and other sweets to top our toast with. Mollie would often be standing by the Aga, checking to see if her socks had dried from the night before. She hung them on the Aga rail to dry, and encouraged us all to do the same. 'Amazing things, these Agas are. So versatile! Not only can you heat the house and cook a three-course meal but you can do your laundry at the same time. Bloody marvellous,' she would laugh.

Before I could offer any sort of acknowledgement, she would slam a fresh pot of strong hot tea in front of us, waving to the pot with her left hand and signalling drinking with her other. 'Drink up, girls. You must be freezing!'

I loved Mollie. She was a wonderful woman, with kind eyes and full lips. Her red hair was swept into a messy bun and she was always wearing an apron, probably because whenever we saw her she was in her kitchen cooking for us.

One morning, the girls and I were sitting having

breakfast as usual. For a change, I had chosen some cereal rather than toast. The girls were chatting among themselves and Mollie was listening to the radio.

'Your caravan's on fire,' a male voice said from behind me.

I looked around the table. No one had stopped chatting, and Mollie was still listening to the radio whilst pottering about.

'Your caravan's on fire,' he insisted.

I looked behind me and saw nothing. I knew I had heard this voice but could not make out where it had come from, so carried on eating my cereal.

'Your caravan is on fire!' the male voice demanded.

I jumped up, and everyone stopped to see what I was doing. I went outside to look without saying a word, whilst they carried on eating their breakfast. I suppose I thought I was imagining the voice. But then I saw Steve coming towards me with a look of horror on his face. We both noticed at the exact same time that my caravan was indeed on fire. And now I knew the voice was real.

What happened next was so scary. Steve was shouting for help as there was a row of six horses adjacent to the caravan and a huge barn that could have gone up at any moment. Everyone came running out of the house, wondering what was going on.

Bang! The caravan blew up before our eyes. The flames reached high into the sky, flaming in colours of gold, orange and red. It was quite a sight to behold. The flames were dancing around almost as if to entertain us. We girls were frozen on the spot for a few seconds, staring up in disbelief at the inferno of flames rising from the caravan. The windows had been blown out by the explosion, so flames were not only coming from the top of the caravan but darting through the windows too. And cinders were landing around our feet.

'Quick! Get the water!' I heard Steve shouting. He and a few others managed to put out what was left of my caravan with buckets of water, and the rest of us hurried the horses out of their stalls. They were shaking with fear but thankfully the flames hadn't reached them. It really was a close call to both the stables and the barn going up in flames.

The strange male voice that alerted me that morning had saved the lives of those horses. I was so very grateful – but I didn't know who to thank. Who was it? And where was he? Why did he warn me? Was he my guardian angel? I didn't know, and I didn't talk to my mum about it either, even though she might have been able to explain what or who it was. Having been taken to a spiritualist church as a child she knew about such things. But I never spoke to her and I'm not sure why. One thing was sure: the voice was loud, clear and very real.

This was my first clear psychic experience. My earlier experiences were quite subtle: a quiet voice in my mind, a whisper or even a hint of words for me to understand. And always from the animals I was around. This was totally different from anything that went before, such as the times when I knew there was someone or something watching me, making me avoid going to certain parts of our house through fear of seeing a ghostly figure.

Even after all these psychic feelings and experiences I was too young and naive to understand what gift I had. Yes, they were remarkable and odd, but I couldn't explain what they were, or how I could use the information I was able to receive. I felt my intuition was on the path of spiritual growth and that with each day more and more uncanny experiences would develop my ability. I just needed to understand what ability I had.

I spent the next few weeks being scared of my own shadow. My head was full of confusion. Who was it that had spoken to me that morning? Would he come back? Could he see me? Oh, crikey! This was a worrying time for me. I was young and unaware of any real psychic ability, though I knew I had an affinity with animals. But was that really psychic or just intuition? Or is that the same thing?

Heidi suggested I went to a spiritualist church and try to speak to one of the ladies who organised the evenings. I thought it was a great idea. I told Heidi about my mum's experience as a young girl, visiting a spiritualist church with her grandparents on a weekly basis. If my mum could do it, so could I. The following week, after searching the local newspapers for our nearest church, off I trotted.

Once at the church I began to feel very nervous. I'm not really religious – I believe there is something out there, but even to this day I'm not sure I truly know what it is. I suppose I am more spiritual than religious.

Other people started arriving. Some were elderly, some middle-aged and there were even a few teenagers giggling arm in arm as if they were on a night out at a club. They weren't at all what I expected. I had an image in my head of old witch types with crooked teeth and warts on their chins with hairs protruding from them. But no, they looked normal.

I walked in and took my seat with the others. Everyone was whispering, so it was extremely noisy with the hustle and bustle of the people and their hushed voices and giggles. Then all of a sudden, silence! And up on the podium stood a little old lady with a grin of excitement on her face. Her silver hair was neatly combed into large roller-size curls, and on her arm rested a small brown leather handbag.

'Thank you everyone for coming. Could you please put your hands together and welcome Mr John Crabtree.' (Actually this is a fictional name as I can't remember the visiting medium's name, so I apologise to the man if he happens to be reading this.)

There was a loud applause and up jogged a very American-fanfare type, waving and blowing kisses to his adoring followers, all seated before him in rows of five. I found out later that his most loyal devotees often followed him from church to church just hoping to receive a message.

I have to say the messages he gave to people that night were truly moving. Some people were in tears, but so very grateful for the opportunity of speaking with their loved ones. The readings started with Mr Crabtree looking to the ground in silence for a few seconds. Everyone was transfixed by him, waiting for his message. Suddenly his head lifted and his eyes fastened onto a little old lady seated in the second row.

'Hello, my dear,' he smiled. 'Are you OK with me giving you a message?'

She nodded her head keenly.

'Please could you answer yes or no, my lovely. That way I can tell if you have accepted what information I have for you,' he said to her gently. He came across as charming and kind, and I liked the way he made people feel at ease and not scared.

'I have your husband with me,' he said.

I heard a lady directly in front of me whisper to her friend, 'Hmm. Anyone could say that. Let's face it, she is ancient!'

'Shh,' a man began, angry at the women for interrupting the performance.

Mr Crabtree never noticed; he was focused on his subject. It was as if all outside interferences had disappeared and he could only hear the voice of the spirit, his own voice and that of the little old lady he was reading for.

'I have Henry with me, my love. Yes, Henry is here.'

The little old lady smiled and said out loud, 'Yes, that's my late husband.'

He then went on to describe exactly what Henry looked like, with the lady agreeing that all the information was correct.

'He is laughing. He is telling me you went out this morning with odd shoes on. He is laughing because he says it wasn't until you got to the post office in the high street that you noticed. Is this right, my love?'

Everyone turned to look at the lady, who was in fits of giggles, barely able to get the words out through her laughter. She explained he was quite right; she had been all around the town doing her shopping before she stood outside the post office, looked down and saw she was wearing one black shoe and one brown. The shoes were identical in style but two completely different colours. The hall erupted with laughter. It was a real moment of validation for all.

Mr Crabtree went on talking with Henry, her late husband, who proceeded to talk about matters that only she and he knew. The little old lady looked as if she had been covered with a warm blanket of happiness and love. Her cheeks had colour and she was smiling from ear to ear.

'Thank you, my lovely. It was a pleasure working with you. I will leave Henry's love with you,' he whispered, gently smiling at the lady and then at his adoring public, who were transfixed in amazement at his connection with the spirit world.

To say it was pretty impressive would be an understatement. He must have read for around ten people, with accurate results every time. I learnt something very important that evening: messages from loved ones who have passed over to the spirit world can really bring peace and tranquillity to their receiver.

At the end of the service, the lady who was hosting the evening thanked the medium for his contribution, and said that if anyone had any questions they should see her after everyone else had gone. Here was my chance. I felt a little nervous waiting in the queue, but hopeful that my questions would be answered.

'Hello,' she said. 'What can I do for you?'

I smiled at her and explained the story of the male voice I had heard and the fire.

'Oh, goodness. That must have been a shock. But there's nothing to worry about. It's just your spirit guide! We all have them.' And with that she spun round on her heel and began to answer someone else's question.

Spirit guide? I thought to myself. I've got a guide? So why have I never heard him before? And when will I hear him again?

Chapter Four

My life was changing. Will and I split up. We were arguing about silly things, such as not seeing each other often enough and me being too busy to make time for him. An overwhelming sense of gloom came over me as I felt a shift in my world. He wasn't to be part of it. I wanted to be single, on my own. I didn't want or need a boyfriend. I needed to find out about myself: who I was, what my direction in life was to be, and where I saw myself in the future.

I turned to the animals for support. They gave me the courage to go forward with my life and to learn new things, especially about the psychic realm. I read books and learnt different skills, from crystal healing to angel therapy. Most of all, the animals were always around whenever I felt lonely.

I began helping more and more friends with their animals. I wasn't sure what to call myself because I wasn't a trainer, but I understood what the animal needed. My friends were impressed at the results but didn't really want to understand how I knew what I knew. So I kept quiet about my psychic ability and my guide. I began to realise that it was probably my guide who was unlocking my ability and that my willingness to accept it into my life seemed to open me up even more than I could have imagined.

Steve had asked if I could work with a rather angry piebald mare. She was bad tempered and very naughty, and few of the grooms would go near her, but Steve knew I might be able to calm her down. I remember putting her bucket into her stall and saying in my mind, I wish I could find a way to pack my job in. I was thinking about leaving the stables and returning home, but just couldn't pluck up the nerve to tell Mollie and Steve. They had been so good to me that I almost felt obliged to stay. But as they say, be careful what you wish for . . .

I jumped as I heard my boss's voice shout over to me, 'Joanne, give her twenty minutes and then could you tack her up and ride her. I have a client wanting to view her tomorrow and need to get her ready.'

'Yes, boss,' I replied.

Oh, crikey, I thought to myself. I really wasn't in

the mood for battling with this grumpy mare today. But I followed Steve's order and twenty minutes later took the bad-tempered mare into the indoor arena to warm up. Steve came in to watch and started laughing as he watched her continuously try to buck me off her back. 'Hang on there, Joanne!' he said, whilst I used all my grip to stay on. 'Just pop her over a fence or two.'

Oh, great, I thought. She's going to love this. The mare was already trying to get hold of the bit in her mouth so she could run off with me.

'What is your problem?' I whispered to the mare. 'Could you behave. Please!'

Still laughing, Steve watched as we galloped towards the fence, with me trying desperately to check her pace so that we could jump it safely. She flew at the fence far too fast, but remarkably we cleared it.

'Bloody hell, you silly mare. What are you trying to do – kill me?' I snapped.

'You wish to go home, don't you?' she snapped back, as we approached the fence for the second time. This time I was not so lucky. Right at the last minute she deliberately put in another step and I fell off, landing flat on my back on the arena floor.

'Ow!' I screamed.

'Crikey, Joanne. Bloody get up and stay on the animal. I need her sorted for the viewing,' Steve yelled.

'I'm trying, but she wants me off!'

I got back on and took her round again. Cantering towards the jump for the third time, her pace was better and she seemed to be starting to settle, but just as we approached the fence I felt her change. She skidded to a stop and I flew over her head. With a back flip I landed flat onto the poles of the show jump. The pain in my back shot through my body as I fell off the poles with a bump. Lying on the ground in agony, I remembered what the mare had said about me wishing to go home.

'You OK, Joanne?' Steve asked calmly, offering a hand to pull me off the ground.

'Yep, I suppose so, Steve,' I said bravely, trying not to cry. I so wanted to show I was capable of the task he had given me. I hobbled back over to the mare and climbed up on her once again. We gave the fence one last go, and she jumped it perfectly.

'Why couldn't you have done that before?' I asked, patting her neck.

'You want to go home, don't you?' came the reply.

It wasn't until the next day, when I woke unable to move, that I knew what she had meant. My back and left leg had totally seized. Mollie and Steve called the doctor, who gave me the usual painkillers and suggested I see a chiropractor as soon as possible. The chiropractor was booked for the following day, and I had a course of treatment that lasted a few weeks, but I was not getting any better. The mare had fulfilled my wish. Whether I liked it or not, the decision was made that I was heading home.

I spent the next six months almost crippled. My left leg just wouldn't move and my lower back was in spasm on and off throughout the day. It was horrendous. I was only eighteen and could hardly walk! But I've never been a quitter and I decided to ask the local kennels if I could walk the dogs for free. I explained the situation and they agreed. My next month was spent retraining my leg to walk, and slowly the pain eased and the strength returned. The owners of the kennels kindly sent me on a live-in grooming course in Southport, Merseyside, for a whole month. This was a brilliant opportunity to acquire a skill that would stay with me for ever, and I accepted it with open arms.

Although I adored working with the dogs, I couldn't

help missing being around the horses. But the doctors had warned that I would lose the use of my legs completely if I took another fall off a horse with my back as weak as it was. I decided to carry on grooming dogs whilst I thought about what to do. I was feeling like I needed to go places, see new sights and meet new people. I had really enjoyed my time in Kent and wanted to see more of the country.

After a while my dad offered me a job at the kitchen and bathroom shop he had opened, and I took up his offer even though it wasn't working with animals. The shop nestled in a row of other terraced shops on a busy main road with no parking, which was not ideal for a business, I thought, but it did well. His wife did the accounts and my dad fitted the kitchens and bath-rooms.

I hated the job. All I did was answer the phone and speak to customers about things I knew nothing about and felt no passion for. It was so boring, and I was missing the connection I had with the animals. Their pull was very strong. So one day I took out a map from inside the drawer and opened it up on top of the desk. Looking down at the picture of the UK, I picked up a pin from the desk tidy to my left. 'OK, Joanne,' I said to myself, 'let's make an exciting new journey happen.' I closed my eyes, swirled the pin over the top of the map and, with one flying stab, stuck it hard into the paper. Opening one eye, I looked down to see where it had landed. Scotland. I stared down at the map. I've never been to Scotland, I thought to myself.

I set myself a task. I would ask the next two customers who came in to the shop what they thought of Scotland. The first said it was wonderful, and that I would love it. The other said it was terrible, cold and not a great place to be. So it was a 50/50 split, but I needed a new challenge and I needed to be around the animals again. My communication with animals was getting lost with all the work I was doing with my dad's business. It was time to move on.

In the summer I made the move up to Scotland after landing myself a job at a kennels as the head dog groomer. It was a strange place to be. I had moved to a part of west Scotland where there were very few English people, so I was a bit of a local novelty and everyone looked at me oddly when they heard my accent. The job was only temporary until I found my feet and could set up my own grooming business, which I did after a few months. With my savings of just £300

I was able to buy everything I needed: one pair of second-hand clippers, a pair of scissors, a comb, a brush, some shampoo and five towels.

I was in a small town west of Loch Lomond. The area had beautiful mountain views, with mist rolling over the tops of the hills that surrounded my rented apartment. My little dog grooming business was going from strength to strength and I had my own two gorgeous white toy poodles, Minti and her son Klein. And many wonderful friends. Life was pretty good. I had been very lucky indeed.

Every weekend I would go to our local pub with a couple of friends. Out of hours it turned into the most fabulous waterfront nightclub, and it was always a great girls' night out. We had so much fun. One particular night at the club was going to change my life for ever. After dancing with the girls I caught sight of someone in the distance. He was very handsome, with piercing blue eyes, and he was heading straight over in my direction. He held eye contact as he approached me, and I was mesmerised. It was as if we were suddenly the only people in the crowded room of partygoers.

'Hi, my name is Paul. Can I buy you a drink?' he asked politely.

'Yes, thanks very much. A gin and tonic would be lovely,' I replied.

I couldn't believe how gorgeous he was. I had never felt anything like this before. My heart was skipping a beat! We spent the whole evening together, staring into each other's eyes and whispering sweet nothings. As we stood on the decking, looking over the calm water at the back of the club, he took his jacket off and placed it over my shoulders to keep me warm. That was the moment I knew I was hooked. I had fallen in love.

Paul turned out to be a sailor. He came to see me whenever he was on leave and I visited him in Portsmouth, where he was based, at every opportunity. We were smitten. My first true love was something more spectacular than I had ever imagined possible. Paul had grown up on his family's farm, so luckily for me he adored animals. He also rode horses and had even been picked for the British eventing team when he was a young boy. Our relationship was perfect. I couldn't imagine life without him. He was the one! When we were apart my heart ached, and when we were together it beat so fast it hurt. I loved his tanned skin, the manly scent of his aftershave, his soft and caring ways, and his old-fashioned chivalry, such as opening doors and always making sure I was looked after. He was so special to me. And like nobody else I had ever met before.

We spent our holidays in France with his parents, who lived out there since selling their farm – me lounging on the sunbed by the pool with a glass of rosé, whilst Paul read the paper through his shades. Life was idyllic. And I loved it. Soon we were making plans for me to leave my business in Scotland and move down south, to be nearer to France. We hoped we might buy a little property out there for ourselves before too long. I never had any second thoughts about giving up my busy little salon, or the animals I worked with. I was sure that I would always be around lots of new animals and I wanted to be with Paul, no matter where it took me. I remember just telling my clients I was leaving and that was that. I had started up my business simply and I ended it simply. No fuss or regret. I suppose I could have sold the business quite easily, but at the time I wanted to leave quickly. So I packed up and took a job as a nanny, looking after two adorable children in the south of England.

Minti and Klein settled well, and so did I. I had left some really good friends behind in Scotland, but soon made new ones, which made the transition a little easier. And my connection with animals started to come back. The job I had taken was situated conveniently on a polo yard. I had watched videos of polo and loved it, so actually being on a yard and being able to learn how to play was magnificent. I had always liked children and they always seemed to like me, so it was an ideal job. My employers were lovely too, and their children – a five-year-old blond boy called Billy and a gorgeous white-haired three-year-old girl called Petal – were adorable. I was able to play polo whenever I wanted and spent most of my free time playing chukkas and walking the dogs, who loved the freedom of the countryside and warm air. I was living my dream, with horses, dogs and children. And the love of my life was visiting more than ever.

During the time at the house with the children, I never had any connection with the spirit guide that had spoken with me in my teens. Perhaps this was because I didn't need him. Maybe guides only come to you in times of trouble. And to be honest, he was the last thing on my mind. However, I was still helping friends with their animals, sometimes to correct bad behaviour, other times just to find out why their animal was sad. Animal communication has taught me that animals are far more intelligent than we imagine. We are only touching the surface, and I believe that in time we will fully appreciate their potential. By communicating with animals we can understand their needs and wants, their dislikes and likes. Don't you think this is important? I certainly do. By listening to the animals we can unlock the secret of their desires in life and find out what they have always wanted to do. Who is to say animals don't like to have a purpose in life? I am convinced they do, whether it's a job of some description – such as guarding, training, or even just looking after their family – or taking part in an activity they enjoy. Shouldn't they have a right to this?

A lot of racehorses are sent to slaughter once their career is over, and one of my new friends, Arianne, was making a career for herself by retraining them as polo ponies, giving them a second chance in life. She had recently bought a horse called Mr Nice Guy at a horse sale. He had never made the grade as a racehorse, but the world of polo suited him perfectly, much better than racing. He really found polo exciting, and became pretty good at it too.

Arianne was thrilled at her handsome new

companion and friend and I drove over to see them the following weekend, loaded up with packets of Polo mints and carrots, which most horses love as a treat. I arrived early on Saturday morning. The smell of horses and fresh air wafted through my senses, and it felt great just to be outside and around the horses. With a smile and a hug, Arianne invited me over to the stable where Mr Nice Guy was resting. He must have heard us coming because out popped his head over the stable door, and he greeted us with a whinny of delight.

'Wow! What a beauty, Arianne,' I said, grinning from ear to ear like a Cheshire cat. Mr Nice Guy was a fabulously handsome dark bay gelding, who stood around 15.3 hands high, which is actually quite large for a typical polo pony (on average they range between 15.0 hands and 15.2 hands in height). My heart sang with the melody of utter love.

'He sure is, and I am so glad he's with me. He is exactly what I was searching for.'

I couldn't get my hand out of my pocket quick enough. Mr Nice Guy had already pushed his velvet nose into it and pulled out a huge carrot, gulping it down whole.

'Well, there's no doubt he likes carrots!' I laughed.

I spent four hours grooming and pampering Mr Nice Guy that day, and I loved it. Many of my most precious memories of horses are about spending time around them, enjoying their companionship, rather than riding them. They really are truly special.

Arianne kept me updated with his polo training; he was going from strength to strength. His first time out to a friendly game of polo was with Arianne's friends. All the ponies went really well that day, including Mr Nice Guy. She phoned me on the way back from the game, boasting about how wonderful he had been. He had played a cracker of a match. I was thrilled for her and couldn't wait to see them in action.

A few weeks later, the buzz was getting around the yards about how good this new pony was becoming. He was beginning to get a reputation as a potential high goal pony, which is a real honour. These ponies love the game, even chasing the ball themselves and being able to turn on a sixpence when the ball changes direction without the rider asking for it. It's all about agility and speed. A really good pony is very hard to find and they play with the best riders. It wasn't too long before Arianne was being asked if Mr Nice Guy could be used in professional games. It was a really great opportunity for Arianne. She was thrilled at his response to her training techniques, and had saved up to buy another horse at the end of the month.

Soon Mr Nice Guy was being schooled by Arianne in the week and then played in matches with professionals at the weekend. This enabled him to gain real experience with professional ponies and as an athlete. He was really enjoying playing the game of polo, which is fast and physically demanding. When horses have been bred and trained as sports animals it is in their blood and they long to play. (My position on an animal having a sporting career is a 50/50 one. If the animal enjoys his sport and is cared for and treated with respect, then I think it's great. But I find it barbaric that some animals are forced to perform a job they do not wish to do, and are treated unkindly. And it should be stopped. I have worked with animals who have asked to stop what they are doing, or to change careers: luckily for them, the owners have listened to their requests. But in my experience if a horse does not want to do something, it won't.)

One Friday evening, I was talking to Arianne on the phone about the latest shopping trip and she mentioned that Mr Nice Guy was going to be practising polo with a professional rider from Europe that weekend. As soon as she said it, I felt a knot in the pit of my stomach.

'Who is he?' I asked.

'He has come over from Europe to train up young stock,' she replied.

I didn't have a good feeling about it. Who was this guy? Why did I feel really uneasy? Mr Nice Guy had been ridden by many riders over the months that Arianne had cared for him, yet I had never felt this unease before.

'Maybe you should find out a little more about this guy, Arianne, I feel weird about this,' I tried to explain.

'Joanne, don't tell me you are doing your hocus-pocus witch stuff again!' she laughed. Like most people around me at the time, Arianne had noticed I had something strange going on but didn't really believe I had any psychic ability. She just found it very amusing. I was fine with that. After all, she wasn't a client (not that I had any at the time) but a friend. Even though I knew something was wrong, there was nothing I could say to persuade her to believe me.

The next morning my stomach was still knotted up with worry and I was in turmoil, wondering what to do. Should I go down to the yard? Or phone? And then, who was I to turn up and interfere? Maybe I was wrong; maybe I was becoming too involved with the pony and being a little over-protective. But I was so worried about Mr Nice Guy that I decided to phone Arianne. I must have tried non-stop for about an hour. She was probably just busy, but I really wanted to make sure Mr Nice Guy was OK. When I got no answer I became increasingly worried and jumped in my car to go and speak with her in person.

It was about five miles to the yard, down winding country lanes. I must have been no more than a mile away, when I saw another horse owner on the yard approaching. She was waving at me to slow down and I had an awful gut-wrenching feeling in my body, a feeling I will never forget. The woman looked as white as a ghost, and not the rosy-cheeked girl I had seen on the yard previously.

I pulled up beside her. 'What on earth is wrong?' I asked.

Her eyes began to well up with tears and a look of desperation came over her face.

'What? What is it? Is Arianne OK?'

'Not really. You need to see her. It's Mr Nice Guy.

There's been an acc—' And before she could finish she broke down in floods of tears.

I drove as quickly as I possibly could to the yard, only to see a vet loading a case into the boot of his car. Arianne was almost being held up by her friend. Both were sobbing and inconsolable. My heart went out to her, but all I could do was hold her. The hurt she was feeling would ease with time, but today she needed to cry.

I knew only too well what had happened. I had seen it all before when young horses were pushed too hard. Mr Nice Guy had been taken onto the polo pitch to practise the new rider's stick and ball handling, and apparently the rider was really rough with him. Most professional players are amazing riders and very gentle, but this one rode in a more aggressive way than anyone who had ever ridden Mr Nice Guy before. When the horse didn't do as he was told, the rider lost his temper and blasted the ball at full swing with his stick. He missed, and with a single swipe the stick went through the legs of Mr Nice Guy. Over the two of them went, hitting the ground hard. The rider got up, battered and bruised, but Mr Nice Guy was not so lucky. To everyone's horror, his foreleg was broken in two places.

Arianne lay with her horse, stroking his soft velvet muzzle whilst waiting for the vet to arrive. Mr Nice Guy was later shot where he fell. It was a dreadful day. No more Mr Nice Guy. He was a wonderful horse whose spirit will always be around, and a tree was planted in his memory.

My psychic ability had warned me something bad was about to happen, and it turned out my feelings of unease about the new rider had been right. My worst fears were realised that day, and now I never ignore my psychic ability. If I feel trouble is brewing, I explore it. I try and find out what it is or how I can stop it, help someone through it or get ready for what may lie ahead. It's easy to spot: I get a deep feeling of dread, my tummy churns and I start to feel restless. These are my warning signs. Soon after I begin to see pictures in my mind, sometimes clear, sometimes not. One thing is for sure, I am now always prepared.

Back at work looking after the children, everyday normality carried on. Paul was due home in just four days' time, and I was thrilled as he was planning to stay four days with me. I missed him so much. He was my strength, my heart. He was more to me than I was.

'Morning, Edward. Beautiful day, eh?' I called over to the chap who lived in one of the cottages on the farm estate where I worked. Edward was a handyman, and had a little sideline business as a wood turner, making bowls and other interesting wooden objects that sold at market stalls. He worked part time for my employer and helped with the horses when the wood-turning business was quiet.

'Morning, Joanne, kids,' he nodded. 'What are you three up to today?' He was smiling a huge grin that almost went from ear to ear.

'Well,' I paused. 'We were hoping you would take us down to the lake to catch some fish.' I was looking down at Billy and Petal. Their eyes lit up with sheer delight. That morning I had packed some sandwiches and small fairy cakes to take with us on our little adventure, and I had put some string and a couple of safety pins in the bag. Neither of them could work out what these were for.

'Sure! It would be a pleasure,' Edward replied willingly.

Edward was a lovely man. Small, stocky and stout,

he had jet black hair and a bit of a tummy that hung neatly over his tatty old brown trousers which he never seemed to change. His job was to trim the horses' feet on the yard and do basic DIY jobs. But on occasions he was allowed to help me take the children out in the grounds of the estate, and elsewhere. I always enjoyed his company and at times when I felt lonely we would share a pot of coffee with a dash of brandy by the fireside in his cottage and he would tell me stories of his younger days. He was softly spoken and really cared about people. He told me that he had an estranged wife who had taken his only child away thirty years previously and wouldn't let him see his son ever again. It was a shame for him. You could tell he had been heartbroken. He had been given a lifeline here at the estate by my employers, with a job, a cottage and, best of all, everyone's friendship.

'This is how you tie the string to the stick and then you hook your pin on the end,' he began, trying to show the children how to make fishing rods. Their little faces were beaming with pride as they threw their fishing rods towards the water, each having placed a small amount of ham sandwich onto the hook first.

'Jo Jo, do you think the fish like ham sandwiches?'

Billy asked, with a puzzled look on his face. (Jo Jo was a nickname they liked to call me; I didn't mind, it was kind of cute.)

'Oh, indeed they do. Edward lost his lunch just last week to the fish, didn't you Edward?' I gave him a wink to agree with my story.

'They did, too. Five ham sandwiches, all gone in minutes. The little blighters!' Edward laughed.

It was a beautiful summer's day. The sky was blue and the sun beamed down onto my legs as I sat on the bank, watching the birds and butterflies flutter about the bushes and trees around the pond. Life seemed perfect. I could hear the children giggling at Edward as he tried to keep them in their positions by the pool of water that was just to the left of a huge pond. The pond was actually full of fish, including freshwater crayfish, but today the pool was the children's fishing ground and they loved it. Personally I would never fish. Fish are animals too, and I do not agree with fishing. I also avoid being present when other people are fishing where possible. However, on this occasion I knew that neither child would be able to catch a real fish with their makeshift rods, so I was sure the fish were safe.

We shared such a wonderful day. Edward loved being

around the children and I adored being around Edward. He always made me laugh and I felt safe with him.

We headed back to the house just as the sun was going down. The children were exhausted but keen to tell their mummy what a smashing day it had been and that Petal had nearly caught a fish. Well, it could have been a bit of weed, but she was convinced it had hold of her makeshift fishing rod and only got away right at the last minute.

'Off upstairs, you two. I will be up in two minutes to get you in the bath,' she said to them as we came through the door.

I was just about to tell her all about our day when the phone went in the kitchen.

'Joanne, would you get that for me, darling?' she smiled.

'Yes, no problem,' I said, and picked up the receiver.

'Hi! Could I speak with Joanne, please,' a familiar voice came down the line.

'Yes, it's me,' I said, knowing it was Paul at the other end. I couldn't help but think it was a little odd. He never normally phoned me at the main house. The next thing I recall was my legs nearly going from under me. I grabbed the chair and sat down, hanging onto the side rail as if I was going to fall off it if I didn't. My face turned white and tears began to slip down my cheeks. I was speechless.

My employer turned to look at me and immediately thought the worst. My face looked horrified, and she began to cry too, thinking it must be something about Paul. Maybe he had been killed in a helicopter crash or some other dreadful accident. She raced over and, seeing I couldn't speak, grabbed the phone off me. I kept hold of the chair, unable to move or speak. To her surprise, it was Paul's voice she heard on the other end of the phone.

'Paul,' she said. 'Are you OK? Is everything all right?'

She winced as he explained how he was ringing to end our relationship. He had met someone else whilst on duty, and they planned to marry.

I was totally heartbroken. I felt my world had fallen apart. I had not seen it coming and neither had friends or family for that matter. We were perfect together. I was ready to spend the rest of my life with Paul.

Shock took over my entire body and the next day my employers swiftly sent me back up to Scotland to stay with my best friend Lyn. She had known both Paul and myself for a few years and I wanted to be with her more than anyone else at the time. I remember stepping off the plane and walking through the arrivals hall, a bag in one hand and a tissue in the other. And there, waiting with her arms stretched out, was Lyn. I took one look at her and almost collapsed with grief.

Over the next two weeks I slowly got my senses back. Lyn helped heal my broken heart by being the best friend I have ever had. She took care of me, listened when I ranted on about him and held me when I cried. I couldn't come to terms with the loss of Paul, but I was just about able to function and get by each day. I never knew love would or could hurt so much. I wanted him back, but in the pit of my stomach I knew this would never happen. He had found his true love . . . and it wasn't me.

I got back to work and kept my head down for a while. I was beside myself with loneliness and I thought about Paul every minute of the day. It was beginning to affect my work: I just didn't have the passion any more. It wasn't anything to do with my employers or the children – I adored all of them and they had been so good to me – but I needed a change of scenery. Too much reminded me of Paul. Everywhere I looked there were little reminders: gifts he had brought me from his travels, items he collected, even postcards he had sent me I would find in my drawer. And when I least expected it the children would ask where he was. So I decided to look for a new job.

Luckily for me a lady on the yard needed a new nanny and within a week I had moved to my new family to care for two lovely boys. My life was starting to feel as if it was moving forward; at last I had a fresh purpose. And my friends stayed close to me. But something quite odd was happening. I began to see more and more of Edward at my new employer's house. He would be there when she arrived home from work, and then turn up at odd hours of the night. They couldn't be having an affair: she was tall and slim, with long auburn hair down to her waist, manicured nails and shoes that cost hundreds of pounds. No, she would never have looked at Edward that way, ever!

Edward didn't seem to want to talk about the subject with me and I found this odd in itself because we spoke about everything normally. This time was different. He began to change and become a bit withdrawn. But he would jump to attention if she even took a breath near him. Just as I had fallen hook, line and sinker for Paul, so Edward had fallen for my new boss – only my new boss played on his affections, getting him to run errands and do jobs for her. When she had been drinking too much he drove her home from parties, and she even let him put her to bed, but being a gentleman he never overstepped the line. He was totally in love, and his heartache was tearing him apart inside. I was getting increasingly worried: she would never look at him in the way he wanted, never. And I know that other friends close to him also warned him off her. But no one could talk him round. His work soon started to suffer and he was earning less and less. Bills were not being paid and he was falling deeper in debt. His failing love life and his ever-increasing money problems were beginning to tip him over the edge.

One Saturday I was due to meet Edward at my old employer's yard to help with the horses. It was something we both loved to do on polo match days and I was looking forward to the hustle and bustle of the day. Pimm's, polo and fit men! After all I was now a twenty-two-year-old single girl and had to make myself get back out there after Paul, and I have to say the guys were mostly gorgeous. But a friend of my boss stopped my car before I even made it to the yard.

'Hey, Stuart. What's up?' I smiled, as I wound down my window.

'Joanne. Umm, I'm not sure how to tell you this. Maybe you should come back to mine and I will explain all,' he said in a solemn voice.

Confused and worried, I went with him straight to his house.

'You had better sit down,' he said, pouring whisky into a glass.

'What on earth is it? What's wrong?' I asked, still confused.

'He's bloody well done it.'

'Who? Done what?' I asked.

'Edward. He's gone and done it this time.'

'What on earth has Edward done now? Is he OK? I was supposed to be meeting him an hour ago,' I said, now feeling rather uneasy.

'I found him. The bloody man has gone and hung himself!'

'What?' I screamed.

'You heard me. He's hung himself.' He took a huge gulp of whisky and gasped as it hit the back of his throat.

'Oh my God! Poor Edward! But why? Why would

he do such a thing? I saw him yesterday, and he was fine. You saw him – he was fine, wasn't he?' I pleaded.

· 'Well, we all know why, don't we?' He looked at me and I knew exactly what he meant. 'She drove him to it. They were arguing last night because she wouldn't let him drive her home. She had too much to drink and he took her car keys off her and . . .' He broke down and began to sob. I couldn't contain my grief. First Paul and now Edward. Why?

I didn't want to go back to the house that night. I didn't want to be in the same room as her. She knew how he felt, so why had she let it go so far? Why? Why? Why? I stayed exactly where I was that night and we drank ourselves to oblivion. Neither of us wanted to face the reality of what had just happened. We held each other and drank as much alcohol as we could before falling asleep.

I had lost two of the most precious people in my life, and my heart was being well and truly wrung out. My boss took Edward's death badly, blaming herself for what had happened and taking her anger out on everyone who was trying to help her, including me. Fuelled by drink, she was hurling abuse at me and her two boys on a daily basis. When she accused me of sleeping with her friends and tried to ruin my own friendships, I decided I had taken enough and made the difficult decision to go home to my family.

Where was my spirit guide when I needed him? I was at rock bottom, and in need of help. My mum tried and so too did my sister Janice, but something deep inside me was burning away. I wanted to punish myself for the pain I had suffered. I blamed myself for letting Edward down, not being able to help him in his time of need. And somehow I blamed myself for the break-up with Paul. I lay awake at night wondering if there had been any signs that I had missed. Had I done something wrong and somehow turned something that seemed so perfect to disaster? I just couldn't get over the continuous turmoil I felt deep inside.

Chapter Five

Needing to pay my way, I found a flatmate and took a job at a local car dealer as a sales representative. It paid well and was pretty secure, but it certainly wasn't my dream job by any stretch of the imagination. I suppose it was a stepping stone. My heart had been broken, I was in turmoil with my life and even putting a smile on my face seemed an effort. This was the first time I actually hated what I was doing. It just wasn't me at all. I struggled to get up in the morning and longed for the end of the day. Selling cars to people, suited and booted, was not my idea of fun. I loved animals, not cars, and I felt totally lost. There were no horses in my life, and my own spirit self was caught up in the world of responsibility. I lacked the love I so desperately needed. Something had to change.

The rain was pouring as I sat at my desk, waiting for the next potential customer to walk through the door. The manager gave us precisely five minutes to approach them or our weekly sales target was increased. This was something I didn't want to happen, so I kept a close eye on the forecourt at all times. I suddenly saw a man and his wife park up their car and begin walking over to one of the cars on the forecourt. Grabbing my clipboard with one hand and brushing my skirt down with the other, I hurried out to close the deal.

'Hi! It's a great car, isn't it?' I said, smiling, and waited for a response.

'Er, yeah. It's actually just what we are looking for,' the man replied.

Bingo! I was going to close a deal here, I thought, and it was probably the easiest sale I was ever going to get. Then, all of a sudden, a feeling of panic came over me. There I was, being a saleswoman in my blue suit (which we girls in the showroom used to call air-hostess outfits, because they consisted of a deep navy blue skirt falling to just below our knees, and a matching fitted jacket), when I suddenly stopped what I was saying and stood perfectly still. 'He's coming,' I managed to say under my breath. The couple looked at me and then turned to each other with a look of bemusement. They probably thought I was nuts!

I pushed my clipboard into the woman's hands and ran towards the main road. It was the A45, a very busy bypass. My boss, wondering what was going on, went to the couple's side. The traffic was zooming up the bypass, but something inside me took over, and the next thing I knew I had run into the middle of the road and was frantically waving my hands in the air, trying to stop the traffic. 'Stop!' I yelled, hoping they would not only see me but also hear my pleas. The drivers slammed on their brakes, nearly causing a pile-up. My heart was in my mouth. Cars were screeching to a halt, with tyres smoking and a smell of burning rubber. By now everyone in the car showroom thought I had completely lost the plot. They just stood and stared at this lunatic in the middle of the road.

Once the traffic was at a standstill, I breathed a sigh of relief. I had put my life in danger. Was I mad? I turned my back to the cars and waited. I knew something was about to happen. My heart was racing, my palms felt hot and my focus started to move onto the noise coming my way. And I wasn't wrong, because suddenly there was a sound of hooves coming towards me from the distance. Out of the slip road, travelling at full gallop against the traffic, came a stunning iron-grey horse!

Everyone's jaws dropped as I walked quietly towards the charging horse. 'Whoa, here boy, whoa,' I called, visualising him slowing down in my mind. (Visualisation is a key technique in communication: you can visualise an animal behaving in a certain way, and sure enough he will pick up on your thoughts and act them out if he is willing.) As he approached, he saw me and almost skidded to a halt.

'Good boy, you are safe now, good boy,' I said, with my heart almost bursting out of my chest. Luckily he had a headcollar, so I took hold of him and waved the traffic on. We were both shaking with adrenaline. I ordered my boss to get a rope, which he did immediately. I did find this funny – I think he was in total shock! And the police soon arrived. They thanked me for stopping the horse and told me later that he had been grazing in a field when a tractor had spooked him. He had jumped over the fence and galloped off in fear, right into the path of the cars on the bypass. If I hadn't had my strange psychic moment, this beautiful horse would have hit the traffic head on at full speed, and what an awful tragedy that would have been. So thank heavens for my psychic ability that day. The incident boosted my confidence: I knew I had a special gift – now I needed to improve and develop it.

I was really starting to miss being around the horses. Their smell, their aura and their gentleness fills my spirit with euphoria. I seemed to spend a lot of my time looking at other people's horses in fields, wishing they were mine. But work was taking over my time, and I didn't have enough money to buy a horse of my own, so I tried to put the thought out of my head. It still didn't stop me reading through the 'Horses for sale' section in our local newspaper. Sitting at my desk one afternoon, feeling bored, I noticed an advert for a shire cross foal for sale. I've always loved heavy horses. They may be big, but they're lovely to ride – something that is often overlooked because of their intimidating size. I had nothing planned for that evening and thought it would be nice to go and see the foal. I couldn't buy it as I didn't have any spare money, but I was interested to see what a baby shire horse looked like in the flesh. So I phoned his people and they agreed to meet me later that day, at around 6pm. I was so excited! Life had been pretty grim recently, but being around a foal would surely lift my spirits.

At the field I was greeted by a really lovely couple

and their three children. They asked one of the children to go and fetch the baby – and out walked the most odd-looking creature I had ever seen. His head looked far too big for his body, his legs were short, and his mane stuck straight up towards the sky.

'This is little Toby,' said the lady, smiling at me.

'Wow! He's unusual looking, isn't he?' I giggled. 'Very cute, though.'

And I do have to admit, as odd as he looked that day, he really was cute. He was very nosy too, hanging around us and wanting to join in our conversation. I had connected with Toby as soon as I looked into his dark eyes; they were so kind. I will never forget the look he gave me that day, a look of love. My heart was telling me, 'Buy him!,' but my brain and sensible side were saying, 'Don't be stupid, you don't have the money.' What on earth was I doing here? I didn't want to leave him behind. I was feeling an overwhelming pull on my heart to buy this foal.

When they asked me how much I would give for him, I very cheekily offered £250, knowing that they wanted £650. I thought this would be my get-out clause. There was no way they would accept a silly offer like that. And thankfully for me, as I didn't even have £250 at the time, they quite rightly refused my offer.

Returning home, I felt really depressed. I should never have gone to see the foal. I was just tormenting myself. I couldn't even afford to buy him. All I could think about was Toby. In my mind, I saw him as he had been when he was first born, then as he was when I met him, then as an adult horse. This ugly duckling was so handsome. I tried to forget him; I tried doing other things, like making a cup of tea and a sandwich, to get my mind off him, but nothing was working. Then my flatmate came home and wanted to know all the details, which just highlighted my pull towards him all over again.

'Can't you just buy him?' she asked.

'Er, no. I don't even have £2 in my purse, let alone £650,' I laughed. 'Anyway,' I said, 'I offered them £250, and they will never accept that amount for him,' and continued to drink my tea. After another twenty minutes of trying to come up with ways of raising £650 and realising it just wasn't going to be possible, I piped up, 'Can you imagine if they phoned and said I could have him for £250?' And before my flatmate could say anything, the phone started to ring. We both looked at each other with amusement, then I dived for the handset.

'Hello?'

'Hi, Joanne. It's Toby's people. We just thought we would let you know we would like to accept your offer of £250.'

I was in shock. Not only did I accept, but I also said I would drop the cash in the next day and collect Toby as soon as possible. I had no money, and no stable or grazing. What was I supposed to do with the foal? Was I mad?

The following day I had to step into gear . . . fast! I borrowed the cash from my dad, found a suitable grazing field with a stable I could use, which wasn't too difficult in our horsey area, and went shopping for some essential equipment. I didn't need a saddle or bridle because Toby was just a baby, so my gear consisted of some buckets, grooming brushes, a hoof-pick for his feet, feed and a bright blue headcollar.

I spent every spare hour over the next few months training him, loving him and telling him all my secrets. Toby was so funny, and he was extremely clever. When the water froze in the drinking trough, the other horses in the field stood and stared at it, almost willing it to defrost, but not my Toby: he walked over and, with one swift bang, planted his huge hoof right in the middle of the ice, breaking a huge drinking hole for himself. The other horses looked totally bemused. They always had to wait until Toby had had his fill before they got a chance. Even to this day Toby is still the boss. He was always first at everything and still is. Feeding, watering, putting his winter rugs on and off, being taken out or brought in from the field, he has to be first. He is No 1, and he lets other horses know this.

As a foal he was cute and naughty, always nibbling my jacket for treats such as carrots and apples. He ate lots and grew fast. And he gave me the love I needed to help heal my heart. We found each other at the exact time I needed him. I was feeling low and the days I shared with him brightened up my life. He was such a pleasure to be around, and I adored him. There was something very special about Toby from day one: an inner knowing of how I felt, a deep connection between the two of us. He was just meant to be with me.

Nowadays, Toby is great at helping me connect to other animals in difficult cases. If I am ever struggling with a reading, I can take the animal's photo over to the stables and ask Toby his advice. Within seconds he will give me the answers I need, acting like a telephone line between me and the animal in question. A little while ago I was trying to connect with a pony that didn't trust humans at all. As a foal he had been traumatised by an owner who hit him around the head with a broomstick. When the owner couldn't do anything with him from that moment on, the pony was sold through dealer after dealer, finally ending up on a yard where a lady took pity on him. She was trying to develop a relationship where, at the least, she could make sure he was wormed, groomed and had his feet trimmed on a regular basis. My job was to get the pony to relax and let these things be done without running for the hills in terror. But whenever I tried to tune in, I felt blocked. He was too scared to allow a connection with a human, and so I asked Toby to help me.

'Toby, how do I connect if the pony doesn't want to?' I asked.

'Offer an apology,' he said, loud and clear and straight to the point.

'What for? I haven't done anything,' I replied, slightly confused.

'For what everyone else has done,' he insisted. 'You have to speak on behalf of all humans. You represent them.'

Oh, crikey! I didn't want to be associated with people that hurt animals. But if that is what Toby wants, that's fine.

'You are not associating with them. You are apologising for your humans,' Toby said, reading my thoughts. This can often happen in conversations with animals. I sometimes think a thought and it will be answered before I have even uttered a word.

'OK,' I laughed.

He was so right. I apologised to the pony on behalf of the humans who had hurt him and promised I would not do him any harm but would treat him with utter respect and sensitivity. Pow! The pony connected. We were suddenly able to converse and resolve the issues that his new owner had been having problems with.

Toby has a knack for being extremely wise but to the point. He is like a grumpy old man in temperament, and now he is growing older it will probably get worse still, even though he's happy enough. His bushy bay coat is as gorgeous as it was when he was a foal. His eyes are as dark as coal and he is more handsome now than he has ever been. He eats too much, always wanting more and more food. This horse really could eat for England! And he does let off when you really don't want him to, normally when I am showing people around the yard. He will take one look at them and push out the biggest raspberry with all his might, for all to hear. So embarrassing! He used to do it when I was grooming his tail, and I'm sure it was on purpose, but I forgave him. He may stink, but he's mine.

He is a lovely ride too, with a bounce like a huge cushioned armchair and smooth as cream pie to ride. My niece Shannon and nephew Billy have both climbed onto his back for their first lessons, and although he stands an impressive 16.1 hands high, he was as gentle as a Shetland pony with them.

Toby is one in a million, even when he deliberately squashes me against the wall with his huge tummy. I would never part with him – I could never part with him. He is my rock. When I feel down, I cuddle him and he cuddles me back, nuzzling my shoulder with his soft muzzle. He has seen me at rock bottom, and brought me back through his love. My horse, my beautiful horse, with his funny little quirks, his wind, his mane that sticks up from his neck. He makes my tummy flutter when I see him, my eyes well up with love when I'm around him and my heart almost leaps out of my chest when I hear his whinny, which he always does when he sees me. I truly love this hairy, stinking, sometimes bolshie, gorgeous hunk of a horse with all my heart. Toby and I have unconditional love at its best.

When I first met Toby I was twenty-three years old, with the world at my feet, but my heart was still in turmoil. I just couldn't get over Paul, and the loss of Edward played on my mind. I even went along to the local spiritualist church to see if Edward would contact me, but he never did. Everyone else in the church would get messages, but me, nothing, though we had been close friends. No spirit guide, no Edward, no nothing. I felt so alone. Even Toby's love wasn't enough. I was soon to press the button of self-destruction.

I felt I needed to do something radical, something that would be totally out of character, and boy that's exactly what I did. The self-destruct mission I was on in my mind was a way of punishing myself. How could

Paul have left me? How could Edward have died? Perhaps it was because I was not there for either of them when they needed me. I felt I had let them both down. I felt worthless.

I remembered seeing an advert in my friend's newspaper, for dancers to work in Vienna. I flicked through the paper and found the ad. It read: 'Dancers required, full training given, no experience necessary.' Well, I had a passport, and I could dance. At the time I didn't know what sort of dancing would be required, but I was willing to try. So I phoned the number in the ad and agreed to meet the organiser the following weekend in a bar. I didn't tell anyone my plans. At the time I felt I needed to go and do my own thing.

'Hi! My name is Shelly. You must be Joanne,' the lady smiled. She was tall, blonde and very slim. She was wearing bright red lipstick and had a beautiful smile that I just couldn't take my eyes off. She was so glamorous!

'So what makes you want to be a dancer, Joanne?' she asked politely.

I wasn't really sure, to be honest. I think it was the fact that I would be running off to Vienna – a new city, a new life and a new me – that appealed, and not the dancing at all. I needed a change of career and a change of direction. I needed to distract myself from the hurt I felt inside.

'Umm, I like to dance,' I replied. 'And I'm willing to work really hard.'

She explained that the contract was only for four weeks. All board and lodging would be paid for and I would get a good wage, too. When the contract ended there was a possibility I could travel somewhere else and work there if I wanted to. She explained that I would be working in a club with another girl who came from Edinburgh. I remember smiling and not asking any questions. I just wanted her to say yes, I could go. So by the end of the interview I was still unaware of the exact details. I knew I was going to Vienna for four weeks to dance in a club, and I assumed I would be working as a pole dancer.

I had seen pole dancers in a club in Coventry I'd been to with friends. We were all dancing the night away on the dance floor, but there were also three small round stages, about a foot in diameter, each with a pole in the centre and a scantily clad lady dancing sexily around it, dressed up as a cowgirl or sailor. I could do that, easy, I thought. All I could think was that I would dance at night and in the daytime go to see the Lipizzaner stallions at the palace in Vienna, who were world-famous as amazing dancing horses.

It was all happening so very fast. We were to fly out the following Monday, so I handed in my notice at work and found friends who would look after my animals whilst I was away. I read a tour book about the city of Vienna over and over, and told my family I had taken a job dancing in a nightclub there for four weeks. They weren't too worried because they always trusted my decisions, and had no idea I was so upset inside. In a way, going on this adventure was a cry for help. I was so naive, having grown up in a small town, protected from the outside world. I had never come across drugs, violence or any anti-social behaviour.

My feelings were mixed as I boarded the plane. Something was niggling at me, and I wondered whether I was doing the right thing. But I soon relaxed when I met the other girl, who got on at Edinburgh. She was petite and really friendly. She introduced herself as Rachel, and I liked her hairstyle – a sharp-cut bob in flame red. It was obviously not her natural colour, but salon coloured to perfection. I also noticed her perfect nails, something I admired because mine were always breaking due to looking after Toby. Having my hands constantly in feed buckets and water troughs was never good for my nails. But Rachel had amazing long slender fingers and pink nails with white tips. Neither of us had ever danced before and we were full of excitement and great expectations for our four-week adventure.

Reality hit us hard the following morning. We had been given the keys to an apartment late at night and, being tired, had gone straight to bed. Waking up, I rubbed my eyes as I tried to focus on my surroundings. They were horrible. Dark, basic and unclean. There was a small bedroom that we shared, one living room-cum-kitchen and a toilet with a grubby shower. Trying not to be too disappointed, we got up and went out to search for a local supermarket to buy some basic cleaning products. Walking along the street, we noticed a strange silence. There seemed to be lots of men getting on with their jobs but where were the women? It was a beautiful city, but just a little odd.

We had been told to be at the club at 7pm that evening. We knocked on the side door and were shown to our dressing room. There we met two other ladies, who walked us around the club. It was beautifully decorated in dark red and gold-coloured furnishings, and extremely plush. The barmen were getting ready for the evening's start, adding the last finishing touches, such as straightening chairs, placing the drinks mats out neatly and polishing the poles on stages before that night's customers arrived.

'You, here,' said one of the ladies, pointing to a chair. They both spoke very good English. 'And you, here,' pointing to another. There was a dressing table in front of the chairs, and a large square mirror. Blu-Tacked down one side of the mirror were various photographs of ladies, very beautiful ladies, wearing bikinis of blue, red, white and green, including amazing multi-coloured ones. Only as Rachel and I looked closer did we see that the ladies were not dancing around a pole. No, they were dancing about two feet away from men. One of the photos showed a lady wearing a leopard-print string bikini, with her back to a man who was seated in a chair, grinning broadly and obviously loving the moment. His hands were positioned under his legs, as if he was forcing himself to sit on them so he could resist the urge to reach out to the lady and touch her. The dancer, who was very slim and had golden brown skin, with long blonde hair to her waist, was slightly arching her back, revealing her beautifully toned body to its best. Her hands were held high above her head, stretching her waist flat. She was caught up in the exotic dance and looked so beautiful.

Then reality struck. I turned and looked at my friend. A look of horror came over our faces at the realisation of what these ladies were doing. We had never stopped to ask what sort of club dancing we would be asked to do, but we knew now. Oh yes, we knew. We were to be table dancers!

We had no money, no passports (they had taken them off us for security reasons, apparently) and we had a signed contract to fulfil. We were young girls, stuck in a foreign country, being asked to dance in a tiny bikini that barely covered our privates for wealthy businessmen. Neither of us wanted to phone our families, because they would only worry, so we made a plan. We decided we would do the job we had come to do, but do it as badly as we could, hoping they would send us home.

The first dance was terrifying because I had no idea what to do or how I was supposed to look sexy. I didn't even look like the girls in the photos. Yes, I was slim, but I had pale skin, straight hair, not a lot of make-up and felt about as sexy as a crisp packet! I walked around the club, trying not to be noticed by anyone, praying

I wouldn't be asked to join a gentleman for a dance. Then I was approached by one of the English waiters. 'Hey, that guy over there by the door would like some booty, so get your ass over there quickly,' he snapped quite rudely to me.

I began to shake and my legs felt as if they belonged to someone else as I approached a very smart-looking gent in his late forties. He was French but he said in perfect English, 'I would be delighted if you would dance for me.' The music was already playing and so I just wiggled around, standing about three feet away. I felt rigid with embarrassment, my face flushed and my knees shaking. Trying to look like the girls in the photos seemed a hopeless dream. The dance, if you can call it that, lasted no more than three minutes and, surprisingly, the time flew. The man thanked me and handed me a ticket. It had one word printed on it – Ten. I put it into the purse I was carrying and scampered off to the ladies to regain some sort of composure.

That evening I danced around twenty times for different men, improving with each dance and throwing in the odd sexy move. At the end of the night each Ten ticket was exchanged by the management for cash, that was after the club took off their forty per cent commission. I actually started to enjoy the thrill of being admired. I even began to feel sexy.

It would have been easy to learn the trade well, and probably grow to enjoy the work. But we had a plan to get back to the UK and so put it into practice. Purposely dancing as badly as we could, we were easily the worst dancers there. It's funny looking back, but we really were terrible. Most of the night we just sat and chatted to each other, discussing where we were going the next day. We could do this for hours because nobody wanted to see our dancing. In the day we made the best of our time sightseeing, and at night were totally awful at our job. Obviously the management noticed and it wasn't long before our wish came true. Within two weeks our passports were given back to us and we were sent home, with our airfares paid. For some reason we were put on a plane to Scotland. I'm not sure why, but I wasn't too worried. It was already familiar to me, and I liked Scotland.

Neither of us had made much money in Vienna, and we had spent what little we had visiting the city's art galleries, the palace and other beautiful buildings. Now I wanted to earn enough so I could bring my animals up to stay with me in Scotland. Although I knew Toby and my dogs were safe with my friends, I missed them dreadfully. Deciding what to do next was pretty easy. We had learnt valuable skills from the other dancers in Vienna. We had watched the girls closely as they worked their routines on the stage. They were so glamorous, and amazing dancers. By pretending to be them we had learnt how to be sexy and charming to men, and this was key to surviving the next stage of our journey. Both Rachel and myself took a job at a new club that had just opened and from being purposely the worst dancers in Vienna, we went on to be two of the best in Scotland.

Table dancing is not the most respected job in the world, but I was lucky to be working in a very respectable club, with very strict rules of conduct for both ladies and gents. It may be different for today's dancers, but back then it was very innocent. Rules were rules and were never broken. The stories you hear are mainly not true, and most of the girls who dance are very talented performers who found themselves dancing in the clubs instead of being a dancer or singer in the West End. I also met girls who held down very respectable jobs during the day and danced at night, not because of the earning potential – they already made good money in their day jobs – but because they enjoyed being seen as a woman, feeling sexy, free and empowered. And contrary to popular belief, most girls had steady boyfriends, partners or husbands of many years who totally supported their choice to dance.

Money was soon rolling in. I made more money in a few weeks of dancing in Scotland than I had ever made. I set up a small flat as my home and brought my dogs up to live with me, arranging for Toby to stay with my friends for a while longer.

The hours were great, and the freedom I felt from being relaxed about my body, dressed in wonderful outfits, with fake tan, gorgeous high heels and glamorous hair and make-up, was just amazing. I danced alongside many successful actresses I've since seen on TV shows and even danced for a couple of well-known celebrities such as Rod Stewart, John Leslie (who was then at the height of his career), many famous footballers and even the actor who played Sinbad, the character from the soap *Brookside*!

I came to love the job. In fact, my memories of it are some of the happiest ever. From being a shy, heartbroken young girl, I became confident, independent and very fit. Within a short space of time I was financially secure. I had worked hard to be one of the best and I paid my taxes. The self-destruct button that I had been so keen to press had turned out to be the beginning of the new me.

I was now more than ready to find my career path, as dancing was only a short-term job. The average age for a dancer was between eighteen and twenty-two, but I was now approaching twenty-six. And, to be honest, I had, in the strangest of ways, healed my heart. Maybe not completely, but more than enough to be able to move forward.

I self-studied during the daytime for hours on end, specialising in animal nutrition. I read as many books on the subject as I could lay my hands on and tested myself over and over about the knowledge I was receiving. I found animal nutrition fascinating and started applying for jobs within the pet trade. I needed to get back to the real world. Dancing was great, but I was living an unsustainable life. Sooner or later age would creep up on me, my looks could go and it would be over.

I would often go and visit my friend Lyn when I wasn't working. We would laugh and catch up on life over glasses of Cava, and I loved being around her dogs FiFi and CoCo. Both dogs being standard poodles they just oozed fun, and best of all they loved my dogs too, so we were all happy! One particular weekend I sent Minti to stay with Lyn and her family. She loved spending time with them, which she had often done when I had my grooming salon. Lyn's dad Billy loved Minti, and she him. When he spoke to her, she wagged her tail as if it were a small propeller, ready to lift her off the ground with sheer admiration. They adored each other. Klein, on the other hand, was a mummy's boy, never wanting to leave my side and quite happy when Minti was away from me so he could have all my attention to himself.

When I went to collect Minti one weekend, she sat on Billy's knee and wouldn't leave him. My head wanted her to come with me, but my heart told me otherwise. I didn't hear words, I just felt the feeling of 'let me stay'. Minti wanted to stay with Billy, and I had to respect her wish. If she wanted to come home, she would have showed me, so if she wanted to stay she would also make me aware, which she was doing all too well. No matter how much we coaxed, Minti had made up her mind. I missed her, of course, but I made regular visits, and seeing her clearly so happy let me relax and accept the situation. She had just moved on.

Chapter Six

I now had my flat, and my little dog Klein, and it was a good life. Klein and I were inseparable: wherever I went, so did he. I loved him so much and he loved me. Klein never seemed to miss Minti's presence. Most people assume poodles were originally from France but they actually came from Germany (the breed being called *Pudel* before evolving into what we know today as poodle). However, they did become a very popular breed in France, having been bred down from the large standard size used as gun dogs to toy size, under eleven inches in height.

The poodle's history is quite amazing. A lot of people who have seen them on TV at Cruft's remark on how stupid they look with the big pompoms. But these go back to their gun dog days, when the pompoms were strategically styled to keep the dogs' joints warm whilst they were in water collecting fowl. The pom on the head is for balance, as were the poms on their hips.

The poms on their ankle joints are for protection and warmth, and the huge one around the chest is to keep the heart and lungs warm. So they aren't so silly after all. Today's standards may be scissored to perfection, but they are a true representation of the breed's history.

When Klein was born, he looked very cute indeed, like a little polar bear. He was tiny, weighing in at just eight ounces. Because of the breed's origins, I wanted to give him a German name, so I decided on Klein, which means small in German. He grew to be only ten and a half inches tall, with a bright white coat which I trimmed into a puppy trim, fluffy all over and about two inches long, with a shaved face to show off his best features: sparkling dark brown eyes and a jet black little nose.

I could just afford to pay a local couple to watch over Klein whilst I was at work, so he wasn't on his own too long. My shift normally finished at 1.30am, and by the time I got back to the flat it was past 2am, so Tom and Jean kept Klein until the morning when I would collect him. They were a lovely couple, and had no children, so I suppose Klein filled the void a little. They were so good to him and he loved being with them.

After a few months working at the bar, I began to chat to a regular called Danny. He was tall and podgy, with glasses – not the usual type I was attracted to! But he seemed kind and genuine. Although he had quite a reputation for his bad temper with the bouncers at the club, I never saw it. I presumed it was just a rumour, as he was always a gentleman towards me. Before long we were an item.

We spent most of our time together and I began to notice that Klein would keep out of the way whenever Danny was at my flat. Danny said he liked dogs but couldn't understand why Klein didn't like him. When I was there Danny would try so hard to make friends with Klein, but to no avail. Klein had never acted this way before, and I had never known him not to like any of my previous boyfriends, so it did seem odd. He would lie under the table, not wanting to come out, and stick by my side like glue. Because he was showing signs of being anti-social towards Danny, I put it down to him being jealous. After all, he was my little shadow. Looking back, I wonder why I didn't question Klein's behaviour. But, as they say, love (lust) is blind and I saw nothing to be suspicious about. Big mistake!

One night Danny said he would watch Klein whilst I was at work. I was happy to let him do this, because first, it would save me money, and secondly, I trusted Danny to take care of Klein. I kissed them both goodbye and headed off to work. I had not been there more than an hour when I began to feel uneasy. I couldn't understand why, and carried on with my shift. By about 11.30pm I just felt the need to phone Danny and check everything was OK at the flat.

'Hi, Danny! You OK?' I asked.

'Yeah,' he said calmly.

I couldn't help thinking something was wrong. 'Is Klein OK?'

'Don't know. He went out and ran off,' he replied.

'What!' I screamed. I felt sick. I lived in a busy part of the city. Klein had never run off before and he didn't know his way anywhere. Oh my God, this was my worst nightmare. He was tiny, scared and on his own with all the traffic.

I legged it straight home to see Danny standing on the doorstep, not even concerned. I was in such a state. It was pitch black by now, and busy with the night's partygoers.

Grabbing a lead and some treats, I spent the next

hour shouting his name, asking everyone I saw and begging for help from the general public. I was in total shock. Then suddenly I received a call on my mobile from Tom and Jean.

'He's here!' Jean said.

'Klein? Is he safe?' I screamed.

Klein had travelled all on his own through five streets of heavy traffic in the pitch black to his safe haven! I should have questioned what had happened and why, but I was just so relieved he was safe, and I took Danny's word that Klein had escaped from the lead when he took him out for his evening walk.

Danny purchased a house nearer to his work and later that month I accepted his offer to move in with him. At first it was fine. Klein still didn't like Danny very much but we were OK. But within weeks of our living together I began to feel that Klein was trying to tell me something. He sat and stared at me for hours, and I just couldn't understand what he was trying to say. As the days went by I had an uneasy feeling about Danny. I was now further away from my job, so I had been leaving Klein in the care of Tom and Jean for longer each day. It was easier and I knew he was being well looked after. Now I began to ask

Tom and Jean to take Klein even on my day off. If I wasn't going to be in, I'd drop Klein off at their house.

It had begun to dawn on me that Danny was abusing Klein. I started to piece together Klein's behaviour: the look he gave me when Danny was in the room and the overwhelming fear I felt in my stomach, as if Klein was making me feel his own fear. I felt sick to the bone. Danny was jealous of my relationship with Klein. I suppose I lavished attention on Klein, and this aggravated Danny at times. He would start the odd argument and bring Klein's name up, saying what a spoilt brat he was. I made the decision to leave. It would take a couple of weeks to get enough money together and get organised, but I was out of there as soon as I could get a place to stay.

I realise now that Danny had a feeling something was wrong. He was sharp with me and kept asking why I was keeping Klein away from him. But what happened a couple of days later was the worst moment of my life. Even now, I struggle with reliving the memories and writing this is really hard for me, but I feel it's a very important lesson. Always, always listen to your pets. They are brilliant judges of character and pick up on stuff long before we do. I have no doubt Klein knew full well he was not safe.

At six on a Friday morning I awoke to Danny yelling and screaming at me, 'That bastard dog!' I sat up, Klein at my side. 'What? What is it? What's the matter?' This was a temper I had never witnessed before. He was red with anger. This was obviously the temper that the bouncers had recalled, the temper I had never seen, until now. His veins were bulging, and his chest was puffed up so big I hardly recognised the beast that stood before me.

Before I could even wipe the sleep from my eyes, all six foot of podgy rage leapt to the bed with fire in his eyes, grabbed hold of Klein with his shovel-like hands and threw him hard against the wall. It was like slow motion. I was naked, screaming at the top of my voice for him to stop. I wept tears of fear, not for me but for Klein, as I saw his little body slap hard against the wall. He made no sound.

Somehow I managed to grab Klein before Danny got his hands on him again. I raced into the small bathroom that was opposite the bedroom and locked it. Klein was lifeless. His body was smashed. I was in shock, but a rage only a protector can imagine began to run through my veins. I had to get out of the house. Outside, I could hear Danny screaming for me to bring the little bastard out. He began to kick the door with his foot and then started to bang on it with his fists. I was shaking with fear but knew I had to get us both out as soon as I could.

Suddenly it went quiet. I listened closely, all the time cradling my Klein in my arms, saying over and over to him that he was going to be OK. I could hear Danny in the bedroom. The wardrobe squeaked open, so I knew I might have just enough time to make a run for it. I slowly turned the lock on the bathroom door, my breath as quiet as a mouse, and ran for our lives through the house towards the back door, followed by Danny's heavy boot steps. 'Come here, you bitch!' he yelled.

As Klein and I reached the back door, Danny was behind me. He lunged to grab Klein from my arms and the devil inside me came to the surface. I do not know how, but I managed to fight him off. Somehow I broke free and scrambled out of the door to the yard outside. I knew my only hope was to wake the neighbours and so, with Klein held tightly to my chest, I began screaming as loud as I could. I screamed like I have never screamed before.

It worked. Danny disappeared when I started yelling. A neighbour looked out of the window and saw this fully naked girl and her dog in a state of utter panic, and out she came with a blanket. She quickly wrapped it around us both and took us into her house. Thank God for her! Before I knew it, Klein was being treated by a vet on the living room floor and then taken to the vet's practice and put on a drip.

My whole body was in shock. Seeing with my own eyes what Danny had done made me ill. I spent days and nights sleeping with the nightmares and the doctor offered me all sorts to calm my nerves, but all I wanted to do was make sure Klein was OK.

We both recovered quickly. Danny had broken nine of Klein's ribs, but thankfully he was a fighter and fought his way back to health. When he was X-rayed, it turned out that three more ribs had been broken a few months previously, due to kicking. Yes, Danny had been abusing Klein without my knowledge. My guilt will be with me for ever. Why didn't I listen? Why hadn't I realised sooner what Klein was trying to tell me? I never discussed what happened with Klein himself, because I was worried it would make him relive the horror, but I did say all through his life how sorry I was for not realising earlier.

Even though I had experienced a psychic connection

with other people's animals over the years, I had not fully appreciated that the connection we have with our own animals could be so strong. Animals are able to sense things way beyond what we humans are capable of, and it is so important that you listen when they try to tell you something. When they give you that little nudge with their nose, the bark, or perhaps a paw trying to get your attention, always listen. Always find out what is wrong. I was so busy with work, not getting home until early in the morning and then sleeping most of the day before getting ready to go to work again, that I never asked Klein what was going on. I wish I had.

I buried myself in my studying during the day and danced at night to earn enough money to start afresh with Klein. Toby was still back at home and I dearly wanted him with me, but I needed to get a real job first and build a stable life for myself. A few months passed, my job applications were in and I began to receive some interview dates from various companies within the pet trade. Not only that, but luckily for both Klein and myself, we met my future fiancé Fraser. He was with a friend of mine in our local pub and we just clicked.

Fraser is tall, dark-haired and green-eyed, just like me, and very handsome. He knew about everything that had happened to me, as well as what I had been through with Danny. And, most importantly, he and his family knew what I currently did for a living and were supportive. I truly believe that if you stay true to yourself, are honest and care for others, you will always be respected.

At first we took things slowly. I wasn't keen to rush into another relationship. After all, it had only been a few months since Danny and I had split, and I was enjoying being on my own again. But when someone is right for you, fate has a funny way of throwing in the unexpected. Trust me, this did not happen straight-away. It took a while before I allowed Fraser into my life, and I was obviously extremely protective of Klein at that time. But eventually, I invited Fraser to my flat for some dinner, feeling nervous because I fancied the pants off him.

I heard a knock at my door. 'Oh, God!' I said to myself. It was a difficult time, and he was the first boyfriend after the monster. I ruffled my hair, which was really long in those days, pushed up my boobies (we all do this, don't we girls?) and headed for the door, twisting my skirt straight as I did. I remember thinking, I wonder if he will bring me flowers. I adore flowers. They smell gorgeous and always brighten your day.

I greeted him with a huge smile and, to my surprise, there were no flowers. But what this six-foot three-inch hunk of a lad brought with him that day was a bunch of doggy chew sticks, which he held up proudly and waved in my face. 'These are for Klein,' he smiled warmly. Well, all I could think was . . . He's won me over!

The same could not be said for Klein. He liked Fraser, but when I was out of the room, Fraser told me he could see the memory of the trauma in his eyes. The bad memories had been engraved on his mind. He would hide under the bed, under the sofa, in fact as far away as possible from any male contact. He trusted none of them. Hats off to Fraser though: he spent a whole year and a half coaxing little Klein to trust him, as well as bribing him (with chicken). Thankfully it paid off. The bond between the two of them was incredible. Klein learnt to trust Fraser like no one I had ever seen. We laugh about that first dog chew incident, because Fraser will say he knew my love for Klein was beyond that for any man, and just as a woman would win over a man through food, so he wooed a woman through her dog. It worked!

The three of us spent every hour together and before long we were a real family. Klein adored Fraser, and Fraser Klein. And me? Well, I loved them both. Fraser was fantastic with Klein, always making an effort. Fraser didn't believe in psychic connection with animals, nor did he realise that I had an ability. At the time, I wasn't even sure about it. Watching Fraser with Klein made me realise that some people are just wonderful with animals and others not so. Some people care, whilst others do not. It reminded me of something that happened when I was a little girl.

My family used to keep chickens in the back garden. I remember them vividly. My older sister Julie had a large white hen and I had a brown one. There must have been about twenty brown ones in that hen house, so bearing in mind I was only about two years old, I have no idea how I knew which one was mine. But according to my family, I did. I'm not sure when the chickens arrived at our house, but they had been with us some years when my dad decided he didn't have enough time to take care of them any more, and so felt it would be better to find them a new home.

Julie was devastated, and I, fearing for the hens, wondered what on earth my dad would do with them. A few days later, he announced he had found a home for our hens, explaining that they would be going to one of our neighbours. We were delighted at this news.

'Who's going to have them?' Julie asked, looking relieved, though she was still disappointed they were going.

'Bob. You know – he has lots of animals, and I'm sure they will be fine there.'

Well, Bob certainly did have lots of animals, but just what were they? I don't think anyone knew. He was strange-looking and lived with his girlfriend.

Recently my mum told me about a time when she saw Bob's girlfriend looking like thunder as she walked past our house and found my brother Richard, his friends and me sitting in the front garden, killing ourselves laughing. Mum asked Richard what we were all laughing at, only he couldn't utter a word, due to the uncontrollable laughter. Tears flowing down his face, he pointed to the woman as she strutted away, and Mum clasped her hand over her mouth, trying to hold back her own laughter. Bob's girlfriend had obviously been to the loo and got her long flowing skirt tucked into her knickers before leaving the house. It was the sight of her striding up the road, with her knickers out for all to see, that had sent the children into fits of giggles. My mum did do the decent thing and went after her, to announce her unfortunate situation. And the children also got a telling-off for being disrespectful. But even now, thirty-one years later, Mum recalls it being a hilarious event and still finds it utterly amusing.

None of the children in the area were allowed anywhere near Bob's house, because rumour had it he kept wild animals in his back garden.

'I saw a tiger!' one of my brother's mates shouted.

'Well, I saw a bear!' another joined in.

Maybe they did? Who knows?

The morning before the hens' departure to their new home, I sat by the chicken run in our garden explaining to them that we would miss them and that I was sure we would be allowed to visit them from time to time. My last memory was of Bob and my dad placing the hens in cardboard boxes and Julie crying, whilst I sat watching this weird man, with fingernails as black as coal, lifting my chicken into a box.

Weeks went by until eventually Dad gave in to Julie's

demands for visiting rights to see her chicken, and of course mine too. He agreed he would set a date with Bob so that the pair of us could go and visit our hens in their new home. Excited was not the word. Julie couldn't wait. At last we would see our beloved pet hens again. That afternoon Dad went round to Bob's to organise the visit, and we waited patiently for word. Our dad appeared back just a short time after leaving.

'Well, when can I see my hen, Dad?' Julie said, full of excitement.

Dad's face went a sort of grey colour. I can't really remember anything else apart from Julie screaming and not speaking to Dad for weeks. It turned out that Bob had not taken the chickens as egg producers, as Dad had assumed. Yes, you've got it – roast chicken, chicken stew, chicken sandwiches, chicken everything for two whole weeks. He and his girlfriend had eaten Julie's white hen and my brown one for dinner! That was my first realisation of my innocence about animals and people. Not everyone holds animals in the same respect as I do. The hens that had been our well-loved pets were another man's food for his plate. Do we judge people as we did back then, when Julie and I condemned Bob and his girlfriend as murderers to the local children, or do we learn from it? And try to understand why and how people see animals differently. I sure had a fight in my own mind to understand why anyone would be cruel to them. As for fur farming, that fills me with horror, particularly as there are countries that still skin animals alive. It's barbaric and in my opinion should be stopped immediately.

Life was excellent. I was offered a brand new role as an account manager for a large pet food company, with a company car, phone and a good wage to boot. Fraser, Klein and our new borzoi Mosko all moved into an old farmhouse together and brought Toby up from the stables at home to live with us in Scotland at last. It really was a wonderful place, for us and the animals. We had acquired two more ponies, not only to keep Toby company but also to keep the paddock trimmed. And we decided to adopt some battery hens.

The choice of battery hens was an obvious one for me because when I was just fourteen years old I was offered a Saturday job at a chicken farm near to my home in Warwickshire. I had no idea what the job involved as we were shielded from animal welfare issues such as battery farming back then (and practices have improved over the years with new animal welfare regulations). As a young girl I was just excited at the thought of caring for hens. They had always fascinated me, with their funny faces and the way they walk. I loved their characters and couldn't wait to start my new job.

It was only a ten-minute walk from my home to the farm, down leafy lanes. 'Hi!' I said to the manager of the farm upon my arrival at 7am. I was beaming with a huge smile and just could not wait to meet the hens.

'Morning, Joanne. Are you looking forward to your first day?'

'Very much so. It's really exciting,' I replied.

The farm manager showed me into a barn where he pointed to some blue overalls that hung from a rusty hook on the old stone wall. He advised me to put the overalls on, as the hens would be quite messy. I didn't think anything of this and proceeded to get dressed. Another two women arrived shortly after me, and we made our way over to one of the three sheds on the farm. The sheds were huge and very long with no windows, just some vents to let air but no light through. I wondered at the time where the hens got their exercise, and thought perhaps they had access to an area at the back of the shed.

I was not prepared for what I saw as the farmer ushered the ladies and me into the first shed. He slid the door sideways and the smell hit me. I could hardly breathe! The stench was overwhelming as the farm manager handed me a mask and advised me to wear it at all times in the shed. He turned up the lights and my heart nearly burst with utter sadness.

'Why are the lights turned low?' I whispered.

'If the lights were on, Joanne, they would peck each other to death.'

Oh, this day was going from bad to worse. As we walked around being shown what to do, I could not take my eyes off the thousands of hens who were packed like sardines into a cage no bigger than a large cat box. There were five in some cages, only three or four in others – and then I saw that the fourth or fifth hen was on the floor of the cage dead, being used as a carpet by the others, perhaps to ease the pain from their feet. Some of the hens that were dead were half-in and half-out, as if the only thing was to escape.

'Collect the eggs from the tray at the bottom of the

cages, and place into the egg boxes,' continued the manager.

His instructions were being overlaid by the awful cries of the hens. 'Help me, help me.' 'Let me out.' 'Can you hear me?' My mind was being overwhelmed with the pleas for help, and there was nothing I could do.

'Here's another bloody one!' the manager snapped.

He opened a cage, pushing the three remaining hens out of his way, and pulled out a chicken by the legs. She was barely alive. Oh, it was awful.

'You will find a few in this condition every day. They are no use for me. I need layers, so this is what happens to them.' And before I could say or do anything he wrung her neck. I'm not sure if I was in shock, but I just wandered through behind the manager, nodding at his instructions and all the time watching the hens in the cages, and their desperate attempts to escape.

Once we had been shown around we were asked to carry on collecting the eggs. I picked each egg up and placed it into the egg box with care. At every cage I sent my deepest apologies to the hens for the treatment and told them how sorry I was that I just couldn't help them. Suddenly the realisation came that perhaps my ability to hear the animals was on this day more of a curse than a blessing. It was dreadful. I felt sick to the stomach for their suffering. I just kept saying sorry over and over again, hoping they would understand. Each cage became more shocking. We removed at least twenty dead hens that morning, but thankfully I didn't have any on my row that needed to be killed. It was terrible.

Then I saw something that has stayed with me for ever – a hen with no feathers. It had either pecked itself raw, or another had done it. I remember her just staring at me. She honestly looked like a frozen chicken that was alive. I felt sick to the depths of my stomach. 'I'm sorry!' I whispered to her. The hen's feet were bleeding where she had been standing on the mesh base of the cage, with barely any room to move, huddled together with her three companions.

I finished my shift and headed home. My mum was nearly knocked over by the stench of my clothes. She even made me undress at the back door because the odour of hen droppings, dead animals and all the other smells of the hen shed made her almost throw up. I think mum was as shocked as me.

From that day on I swore I would not eat chicken or eggs, and I can tell you I didn't for years. Today I only choose organic free-range eggs and beg you to do the same.

I never forgot those poor creatures and I had promised to do something about it. OK, it wouldn't be on a large scale, but it would be my bit.

Now, many years later, I read an article about a lady in Devon called Jane who had rescued some battery hens and re-homed them. I decided I would rescue a couple of hens from the system myself. So I phoned round a few of the remaining battery farms in Scotland and was met with a brick wall. No one would give or sell me any battery hens. Most cut me off instantly. Then I spoke to a lady who, although she was very suspicious of my intentions, listened to what I had to say. But still she refused to offer me any hens.

I was stuck. No one would help me. So I sat with my poodle Klein and whispered to him, 'Hey, Kleiny, what should I do?'

'Go, meet her,' I thought I heard Klein say. Was that in my head? At this early stage I still wasn't a hundred per cent confident about my ability, so I still doubted that I really hadn't imagined it.

I decided to take Klein's advice and travel down to the farm in person. As I approached the house, the lady I had spoken to on the phone appeared. We went back over the conversation about me wishing to purchase a couple of hens. And to my surprise she leant close to me and whispered, 'If you come back early next Wednesday, all the hens go to slaughter. My husband won't be here. I will see what I can do.' And with that she turned and went back into the house.

My heart was racing. It turned out that the hens are only in the sheds for fifty-two weeks as their egg production slows right down after that. Then they are slaughtered. The hens never experience daylight or a natural free life. The farmers even have to pay to have them taken away. I was so relieved that at last I could change the life of at least two hens, which was all I had room for.

The morning for the collection came. I was so nervous. How could I possibly go into the shed and choose the two who were going to live? What about all the others? I was filled with strong emotion, a cross between extreme sadness brought on by the memories of when I was fourteen, and extreme happiness that I could offer a safe loving home where the hens could enjoy fresh air, food and water, lie outside in the sun and be free.

I placed a large dog cage into the back of the car and made my way to the farm.

The lady almost stopped my car at the driveway entrance, not letting me anywhere near the shed. I could see she was in a hurry to get the exchange over and done with before her husband arrived home.

'How many do you want?' she shouted.

My heart was beating hard. I would have loved to take all ten thousand of the girls that were at the farm, but realistically I could only house two.

'As many as you can fit in my cage,' I called back.

What was I thinking? I only came for two! But I needed to save as many as I could, for they were facing certain death that day. Before I could change my mind, the lady came out with four hens dangling upside down from their legs and threw them into the back of my car, where they landed with a thump. Shortly after came the next four.

'There you go. Now, get out of here, before I get in trouble!' she said, waving me off.

The journey home was interesting. I had an extreme sense of relief. I looked in my mirror to see eight hens, all sitting in shock at their ordeal. I spent a part of the journey sending comforting loving messages to each and every one of the birds. They were all beautiful, but one hen stood right out. She was in a bit of a state, with some of her feathers missing, but the ones that remained were bright orange. She oozed star quality.

Whilst heading home I managed to arrange homes for six of the hens with friends, so they were dropped off along the way. Three went to one home, three to another, and both homes were just perfect. So I was left with two: the bright orange girl I had chosen from very early on, and another deeper red hen. I now needed names for them, but what on earth do you call a hen? Every time I tried a name like Harriet, Jenny or Mabel, I kept getting a little voice saying 'Princess Laya'. 'Princess Laya' repeated, over and over. No matter what I said, the name kept coming back. I looked in my mirror and the little bright orange hen was staring at me.

'Princess Laya,' it came again.

Princess Laya, I said to myself in my head. I hate *Star Wars* films, I thought.

'Princess Lay-er,' this strange little voice said again.

'Princess Layer!' This time I was speaking aloud. 'Ah, I get it. Layer as in laying eggs!' I looked back at the little orange hen and smiled. 'So your name is Princess Layer then, is it?'

She fluffed her wings at me in delight and plonked herself down for a rest. Who says hens can't talk? And from that moment on, that was her name. The other hen looked just like a Patricia, and since she didn't seem to put up any objections to the name, that's what I called her. Both were so full of character, and we miss them so much now they're gone. They lived nearly three more years after being rescued, and contrary to popular belief, they both continued to lay eggs almost until their last days. They spent hours sunbathing and enjoying the daylight and fresh air. Princess loved sitting on our garden swing seat whilst enjoying a cup of warm tea! They were happy, content and free.

One of the most common questions I get asked is, 'What is your view on eating meat?' Well, I have been a meat eater for most of my life but my views have steadily changed the more I have become aware of the animals' ability to feel pain and suffering. Our family didn't have a lot when we were growing up. We ate what was put on the table, and most dinners consisted of meat. I never connected the meat on my plate with the animals in the field: it took working with the animals for me to associate the two.

I decided to go meat-free at least six times, each time failing when out for dinner with friends. It wasn't that I didn't care about the animals. It was a simple and stupid moment of disconnection. I did not find it easy, although it should have been. Eventually, though, I simply had to do it. I had to commit fully to being a veggie. It was my choice. I decided it was right for me and I succeeded, so now I have the same food but replace the meat dishes with a substitute such as Quorn. My favourite dish is good old spaghetti Bolognese. It still tastes great, but now it doesn't hold any guilt. I haven't quite gone down the vegan route yet. I did try but found it very difficult to do on my own. Maybe one day I will.

I do not think we will ever stop meat farming. My own aim is to persuade the industry to take care of the animals that are bred for meat by making them comfortable and looking after them well, and not using mass production methods. All animals have the right to fresh air and free-range living, good food and a life free from abuse. I believe my energy is better used trying to make meat animals' lives better whilst they are here (through kind farming and stricter transportation regulations and slaughterhouse standards, all of which need lots of improvement) than preaching at meat eaters. In my experience, most vegetarians had a personal moment in their lives that made them give up meat, and that moment wasn't someone preaching at them.

Chapter Seven

The farmhouse was huge, with large rooms and high ceilings. Each room had an open fire, which we tried to use as often as possible as a natural source of heat. The decor was traditional, in colours of terracotta, blues and yellows which lovingly hugged the walls. Each window wore huge extravagant floral curtains, which hung beautifully from ceiling to floor. It was truly homely and everyone loved to visit.

Every room in the house felt relaxed and comfortable, bar one: the sitting room. It never really felt right. For the year we stayed in the house I only sat in there a handful of times. Fraser sometimes asked why I wouldn't come into the room, but I always made an excuse about preferring to sit in the kitchen, or said I was busy doing other things and would be through soon, but never actually ended up in there. I only told Fraser what the problem was after we moved. He is easily spooked. When I walked in I could feel a change in temperature. Sceptics will put this down to our heating, or draughts, but I can assure you that this was not the case. And I used to feel I was being watched. I'd feel ice cold and a sense of dread would come over me. So I just stayed out of the room. I didn't want to know why it felt like that. After all, I had to sleep in the house, sometimes on my own when Fraser was on night shift (at the time he was working as a chemical operator, which he really didn't enjoy, but the money was good and the hours suited him).

Someone had obviously loved the farmhouse once and made it their own, with tender and loving care and lots of hard work. The house was one thing, but the gardens and outbuildings were another. We were just renting, like the tenants before us, but we were the first people in about forty years who actually wanted to use the outbuildings. For us, they were the perfect opportunity to make stables for our horses and perhaps have some goats too. I adore goats. They are hilarious, always getting up to mischief and making me laugh with their funny little wiggly bottoms and inquisitive faces.

The gardens were as pretty as a picture. There were rows and rows of pink and red scented roses, small colourful shrubs, a few different-coloured holly trees and a small orchard of around twelve apple trees. The outbuildings overlooked the gardens, and when we first went to investigate the shabby old brick buildings, it was truly like stepping back in time.

The best and most memorable building was the old stable block. We squeezed through the broken wooden doors and stood in amazement. 'Wow!' I whispered.

'Yes. Wow!' Fraser uttered. The floor was mostly still intact. The cobbles were strewn with cobwebs and dust, but you could still see the beauty in each individual stone. There were five solid wooden partitions down the length of the building, which would have been used to separate each of the horses. Amazingly, they were still in good condition. Hanging on the walls were leather harnesses, bridles and other driving equipment. They were obviously very old and tatty, and the leather was stiff and unusable, but they had been traditionally made, crafted with horsehair. Everything was covered in cobwebs and it was like being in a film set. It was mind blowing.

Each building we entered had its own character, some with old show tickets pinned onto beams of wood, First Prize, Second Prize, Third Prize, Best

Exhibit. My brain was in overdrive, trying to imagine what it must have been like all those years ago. Who lived there? What were their lives like and, most importantly, did they mind us being there? It was a maze of history past. And I loved it.

We soon cleaned up the buildings we wanted to use, and made sure we didn't disturb any of the original features. Strangely, we found at least twelve cat skeletons, including four on the stable floor. They had obviously been there for years, and I couldn't help wondering why. Were they trapped? Starved? Infected with a disease? It was very odd. I felt a little unsettled by the cats, and hoped and prayed they hadn't suffered. But overall it was perfect for our horses. And we soon became the proud carers of two very naughty white goats, called Billy and Margaret.

It's true what they say about goats: they really do eat everything they shouldn't. Margaret would escape from her paddock with Billy in tow, and the pair would squeeze through the fence, devouring the flower beds like two electric mowers, or chewing the washing hanging on the line. They even ate Fraser's underpants! Boy, they must have had strong stomachs. One day I had the morning's mail in my hand as I was walking past the two naughty goats. Before I could even turn to see what had happened, it was gone. Yep, the mail was now somewhere in the depths of Margaret's tummy.

As the weeks went by, Fraser and I had made a good start on the house and outbuildings, and we invited my mum Jean and my nephew Ashlee up to see the work we had done. It was July. The sun was warm and we were looking forward to my family's visit. Mum and Ashlee arrived and instantly fell in love with the place. We had decided to take some photos, so Mum could show my family back home in Warwickshire. Ashlee had the great idea of having a photo with Billy and Margaret, so I took a Polaroid of him standing next to them, with a huge cheesy grin on his face.

As I was shaking the picture in the air, being careful not to touch it, I began to feel a little odd. When I looked at what was starting to appear on the photo, I froze.

'Umm, Mum?' I called. 'Come and see this.' She came over, took one look at the photo and gasped – because there, on the developed photo, were four or five faces. And I don't include Ashlee and the goats when I say this. There was a man with dark hair, roughly in his mid-twenties or early thirties, an older woman in her sixties or seventies, and a few others who were only just visible. There was a red haze around them.

That was the start of something paranormal connecting with me, and soon afterwards I began to feel more aware of a presence in the house. I think Ashlee's arrival may have triggered the ghosts to come out. He was only about eight years old and they seemed to be more sensitive to the presence of young people, perhaps because of the child's willingness to have an open mind. Children have no preconceived ideas of the spirit world and this attracts the spirit's sense of fun.

Another morning, when I was outside feeding the horses, I turned to look over at the house and saw a woman walking from the patio doors of the sitting room, out onto the stone terrace. Then she disappeared before my eyes. It all happened so quickly that I don't even remember what she was wearing, but in those moments I knew for certain that I had clearly seen a ghost.

I always felt they liked us being at the house. We cared for it, as they must have done.

It's quite strange that as a child I was really spooked

at the thought of ghosts being around me, yet now, as my psychic ability was growing, I was relaxed about them. My view on such matters is that there is no need to be frightened of the spirit world. In my experience spirits are just wanting to connect with us. Some of them are residual energy, as it is known in the psychic world; in other words, spirit energy retracing the life it once lived, a bit like a playback on a videotape. If you are not scared of loved ones whilst they are alive, why be scared of them when they are passed? For most people it is the 'unknown' that is the scary part, and not the actual spirit itself. Some television programmes and mediums portray the spirit world as dangerous and not to be messed with, but this really isn't true, in my opinion. If you have a good heart, you will only attract good spirits. No spirit will hurt or scare you; only you can scare yourself. And nine times out of ten, you will only hear or see spirits if you encourage connection. Some people freak out at this connection when it happens, but let's face it, spirits are only acknowledging your request.

We are all connected by love, whether it's the love of people, family, pets or friends, or even homes, places or special events that happen in our lives, so why wouldn't we want to come back and relive those memories after death? We are not coming back to scare people – we just want to make a love link. It makes total sense.

I'd almost forgotten about the voice. It started again, or should I say he started again, when I was a twenty-seven-year-old young lady. I had had many psychic experiences by then, including the ghostly sightings at the farm, and had begun to do readings for friends. More important – at least from my perspective – was that communications with animals were becoming extremely clear and accurate.

I was getting very interested in the world of spirits, mediums and the supernatural, and was absorbing as much knowledge as I could by reading books, watching television programmes and attending spiritualist churches.

It was a normal day. I had some shopping to do and jumped into my little jeep to head off to the shops. I adored my jeep. It was a typical hairdresser's-style jeep, with a white soft top and a pearlised blue body. It was old and didn't cost me much, but was always reliable and handy for my dogs to travel in. I drove to the shops, got my shopping and set off back home. I was one street away when, out of the blue, the voice said, 'He wants to buy your jeep.' It was him again, my guide. I recognised him straightaway. The tone of his smooth soft voice was familiar. There was no mistaking who it was. I could hardly breathe.

'What?' I gasped, trying to keep the car on the road.

'The man wants to buy your jeep,' he replied.

Nothing else was said. I pulled into my driveway, parked the jeep at the side of my house, and began to think I had been hearing things. Spirit guide? Really . . . it's only taken him nearly ten years to speak to me again! And so I chuckled to myself and went into the house.

I was in no longer than ten minutes when there was a knock on the door. Thinking nothing of it, I opened up and saw a strange man standing before me.

'Hello. Can I help you?' I smiled.

'I would like to buy your jeep. Would you consider selling it to me?'

I remember staring at him in shock. 'Er, thanks, but it's not for sale,' I mumbled, and closed the door. We lived at the end of a quiet cul-de-sac, where you could not be just passing by. It was very weird.

'The voice! The voice! It is real!' I gasped, as I slid down to the floor, my back against the wall. I was in total shock.

Two weeks later, Fraser was mowing our lawn at the front of the house, when I was again popping to the shops for some milk. Before I'd even got to the end of the street, the voice spoke to me again.

'He's cut the cord.'

'Oh, it's you again,' I said calmly, and this time I turned my jeep around and headed home, to find Fraser standing on the lawn with his hands on his hips looking all flustered.

'You'll never guess what I've done,' he said sheepishly.

'Umm, I bet I can. You've cut the electric cord, haven't you?' I laughed.

'How on earth did you know that?' Fraser asked, looking confused.

'Let's just say, a little birdy told me!' Well, guide actually, but I wasn't going to tell Fraser this just yet. I knew it would upset him. He had always been spooked by my psychic stuff and had chosen not to get involved, so for now I was keeping my guide to myself.

After that, I learnt to accept my spirit guide, and even found out his name. I kept asking, 'What is your name? Please, tell me your name,' and to my delight an answer came back. His name was Alan. I felt a shiver of excitement as he spoke the word Alan. I know it isn't a very exciting name. You would think it might be something spectacular like Abraham or Raphael, but no, my guide is just called Alan. He is never with me long enough to ask questions about who he is, or where he comes from. He rarely contacts me, and it seems that I can't call him up as yet. I can talk to him in my mind, but his appearances as the clear voice I hear or have heard in the past seem to be on his terms, as and when he decides. Maybe someday he will tell me all about himself. It's something I would love to hear.

My psychic awareness was growing stronger by the day – not long before this I had been given some Tarot cards and quickly learnt how to use them – and so I carried on doing more and more readings for friends and family. I was even invited to be on the platform at a Glasgow spiritualist church. Lara Wells, a very good friend of mine and a really brilliant psychic medium, was performing that night and thought it would be great if I joined her. She knew I had no experience at platform work but felt it would do me good to get up on stage and put some of the psychic skills I had been learning to the test. I was really nervous. Thoughts kept running through my head like, Oh my God, what if I get nothing? And, I'm going to be standing on the stage looking like an idiot.

I turned up that evening with a tummy that was doing somersaults, contemplating telling Lara that I was backing out. I'm normally quite a confident person, but that night I felt like I was going to be curled up on stage with a dunce hat on the top of my head. The church was warm, with rows of neatly spaced chairs on which were sitting different types of people from many different walks of life, all getting ready to watch the show. I kept myself right at the back of the hall so as not to be noticed by anyone, still contemplating whether I should go through with it or not. The next moment there was a commotion and people's heads turned expectantly towards the door.

'Look, Mum. It's Lara Wells,' a young girl in front of me said, pointing to a flame-red-haired lady almost gliding through the doorway into the room. Of course, Lara looks amazing as well as being bloody brilliant at the work she does.

'Evening, everyone. Nice to be back,' Lara began, as she made her way up onto the stage. I could see everyone's faces light up with anticipation of the night's performance. The leader of the church, a man in his fifties, welcomed Lara and said a prayer that most people joined in. Then, just as they were about to get started, Lara caught my eye at the back of the hall, smiled and said, 'Ladies and gentlemen, I'd like to welcome a friend of mine who is going to come and do a few readings up here tonight for you. I hope you will be kind to her. Welcome, Joanne Hull!' Lara put her hands together and clapped me up onto the stage.

I couldn't help but wonder whether people wanted me up there on stage. After all, they had come to see Lara, not me. My whole body began to tense with trepidation as I looked down at the faces looking right back at me. I noticed a man in his late forties staring at me with no expression at all, just fixing me eye to eye. I blinked, hoping he would avert his eyes, but no, he was still staring. Oh no, this is going to be a disaster, I thought to myself, trying to smile and look like I was OK with it all.

'Relax, Joanne. You will do just fine, trust me,' Lara whispered. 'Let me start, then after a couple of readings, if you are ready, I will hand over to you. OK?'

I smiled at her with a desperate look on my face. What the hell was I doing? Had I gone totally mad? Could I really give messages to random people from loved ones who had passed?

Time would soon tell, because it didn't take long before Lara was coming to the end of her readings. Something strange was beginning to happen to me. I started to feel warmth in my body, and my muscles, which had been as tight as a coiled spring, began to relax. My heart started beating faster and I felt tingling in my hands. I recognised the signs of psychic connection, the same connection feeling I get when tuning into the animals. I started to feel drawn to the seats on the left-hand side of the room, and not only that, my eyes were being guided to a young lady who was watching Lara. I felt strangely drawn to her.

'OK, honey. I will leave it at that. He's leaving me now,' I heard Lara say to her subject. 'Go, girl!' she said, looking at me full of confidence.

The word 'help' rang through my head as I turned to look at the lady I had been drawn to. Suddenly it was like everything else in the room had disappeared; I was totally focused on the girl.

'Hello. Are you OK if I bring someone through from the spirit world for you?' I asked her.

'Yes, thank you,' she replied.

Wham! It hit me: I had a feeling of chest pains, breathing difficulties and trouble speaking. I tried to compose myself as the room held its breath in utter silence. You could have heard a pin drop. I felt the presence of an old woman, a woman who had passed to spirit who was connected with this lady. Who are you? I whispered in my mind. Mother, I heard. It was faint and sounded elderly. It was not a voice that I had heard before.

'I think I have your mother with me. Did she have chest pains and trouble breathing?'

The lady nodded.

'She couldn't speak towards the end, could she,' I said, now feeling more confident about the information I was receiving.

'That's correct,' the lady replied.

Snippets of information kept coming into my mind.

I began to smell her perfume, a sweet floral kind, and could see in my mind's eye how she used to wear her hair. As I relayed the details, the lady kept saying, 'Yes, that is correct.' I felt like I was really helping to bring two people together again. It really was beautiful. The old lady in spirit that I was connected with went on to tell the daughter lots of very personal things which she could validate. With a few tears in her eyes, she thanked me for contacting her mother, and said how much of a relief it was to know that she was safe and well.

The room began to clap and, to my astonishment, as soon as I had finished the first reading I was drawn to another person. It was a man this time, sitting quite near the first lady I had read for. Again all the information came through very easily and was validated as correct. I was not as entertaining as Lara: she was a real pro, making her readings fun as well as informative. No, I was just stumbling through, but doing an OK job for a first-timer.

Soon Lara took over to do a couple more readings before the close of the night. I can't lie and say I wasn't relieved because I was. I decided there and then that it just wasn't my cup of tea. My work was with the animals. I had enjoyed the night, but decided to let Lara and all the others work with people. I just prefer animals. I was and still am a quietly talented psychic medium. I see and hear spirits, but I choose to work with animals. I felt in my heart that my future was absolutely going to be working with animals first and then humans.

But my frustration with my psychic direction was beginning – my focus began to get blurred. People who knew me wanted me to do human readings for them. I had an uncanny knack of correctly getting information for them through my intuition and feeling their emotions as crystal clear, but all I really wanted to do was help the animals. Reading for people is fine and dandy if that's what you do but I was always drawn to use my ability with the animals instead.

The connection with my own animals was undeniably strong now. Everyone who saw me around them just knew there was something special between us. I seemed to know what they wanted, needed and felt, all through a natural connection. I could also feel the connection through other people's animals. It fascinated me. Why could I see there was something more, but no one else seemed to? It used to wind me up so much when people would say flippantly, 'Oh, it's just a dog.' I wanted to scream out, 'No! It's not "just" anything. It's a living, breathing, feeling animal.' But no one seemed to understand. 'If you would only listen,' I wanted to say.

I wondered how I could develop both aspects of my work. My ability was growing day by day. At this stage doing readings for people was purely a hobby, but each time I did one I found my senses getting clearer. I would sit next to a person and begin seeing images in my mind, like watching a video playing. The images might be of someone brushing their hair, or perhaps a lady pushing a pram, or even someone being beaten by another. They were clear and in colour. I was also developing spirit visions. I could see them clearly, but found hearing the voices difficult. This wasn't too much of a problem, because I would just feel the emotion and interpret what they were trying to say. It was always pretty accurate.

I believe that spirits are just souls that have passed over to another place when we die. The link is love, and love is the link. This is what I call the love link: we connect through our love for one another. Spirits are always with us in some form, whether just watching over us or actually visiting from time to time. Either way, we have the comfort of knowing that we are always loved. Some psychics claim they know where people go once they have passed to the other side, but I believe none of us will ever know where the other side is until we go ourselves. For some reason we are not meant to know. And I accept this. In fact, quite honestly, I do not wish to know. I like surprises! Not knowing all the facts about the afterlife doesn't make it impossible to connect with it. I contact the spirit realm regularly, both with humans and animals, and the love we share connects us all.

I often thought about Alan, my guide. Why hadn't I heard him again? Was he really a spirit? And would he ever talk to me again? I didn't know who he was. There was no love connection; indeed, no connection at all really. Just a voice.

Animals are different. If we love animals we can connect – it's that simple. I can hear their words through my own interpretation of what they are trying to tell me. I may see pictures in my mind that the animal is trying to show me, or even video, which is the same as the pictures but in motion. I may even feel the emotional vibration of the animal, which can often bring me to tears. My conversations with the animals were wonderful. It was new and exciting to actually accept I was connecting. I still didn't understand how I was doing it, but I knew I was, and that was all that mattered.

My job as an account manager for the pet food company was taking up a lot of my time, but I tried to have a chat with as many animals as I could, including my own. The goats were funny. They would look me right in the eye and I would get a feeling they were saying, 'If you don't get us food now, we are going to do something naughty', and, sure enough, if I didn't get their food double-quick, they would be up to no good within minutes. Maybe it would be easier to work with humans: they wouldn't eat my washing, or chew through my order pad for work.

I was really excited about the prospect of exploring how far I could take my ability. I was regularly having really good connections with my animals. I was able to tame one of the ponies we had bought to keep Toby company. When I say she was wild, I mean really wild! I spent days talking to her, sending her images of me stroking her head and allowing me to groom areas she wouldn't let people near. Just when I thought she hadn't heard a word I had been saying, she walked over to me, dropped her head and allowed me to groom her. She had heard me. It was amazing! It made me feel alive. But when I told friends of my conversations with the animals, they would smile and make jokes and say things like, 'Ooh, Mystic Meg returns!' and laugh it off as me being slightly nuts. It didn't really bother me. I couldn't explain what I was doing anyway, and would often laugh about it myself. At times I was a little embarrassed to admit my thoughts on the subject. I had only ever heard of human to human readings, and I thought that people with psychic abilities were not meant to speak with animals, that this wasn't part of what they did.

The ways I communicate with animals have stayed the same throughout my life. I have been able to develop my skills to a more accurate degree over the years, but the connection process that came naturally to me is the foundation of the communication that I teach to others today. I still don't fully understand the process, but I find there are four main categories.

1. Pictures
This means seeing a picture like a photograph in your mind. As an example, I remember reading a friend's

cat called Phillip. She said he kept meowing at her cupboard but she couldn't understand why. I decided to ask him what was wrong. Tuning into Phillip was pretty easy. As with all the animals, I noticed the changes in my body first, the warmth and the tingling; then came the shift in focus. Once I felt connected, I asked him, 'Why are you meowing at the cupboard, Phillip?'

'I need oil,' he replied.

'What oil? Is there oil in the cupboard?'

Suddenly I had a photograph in my mind of a star. It was yellowy gold in colour and shaped like a star you might draw. Then I saw another picture, which looked like a plant. A star and a plant seemed a bit odd. I couldn't quite understand the connection.

'Why do you need this oil? I asked him.

'For my health, bones and brain.'

I thanked Phillip for his information and asked his owner if there was indeed oil in the cupboard. She searched through, calling out what was in there. All the time Phillip sat staring up at her in anticipation.

'One tin of sardines. One tin of tuna. He likes those, Joanne,' she said, as I heard the tins clanging around in the cupboard.

'No, he definitely showed me a picture of a star and a plant,' I replied.

'Umm, I don't think I . . . Aha, here are some starflower oil capsules!' she announced.

I was amazed. The pictures represented starflower oil. Phillip had known he needed this for his health. Not only that, but he could quite easily show me in picture form.

Receiving pictures is a fabulous way of communication. Sometimes it takes a little detective work to figure out their meaning, but it really is one of the easiest ways to communicate with your animals.

2. Video

In this case you start with a clear photographic image in your mind. Let's say it is a picture of a black cat lying at the bottom of a bed. At first you see it as a still picture, but if you look closer, you may be able to see the cat breathing. Perhaps his body will stretch out, or he might begin cleaning himself. In my experience, the pictures I see are moving nine times out of ten, and this is what we call video. Most people who choose to develop their natural psychic ability will receive this from their animal at some point.

3. Emotion

Whatever the animal is feeling, you will feel. This may be very subtle, or it can be so strong you just cannot control the tears. You may feel sad or in pain, frustrated or even angry.

On one occasion, I tuned into a horse from a local stables. The owners said she was acting strangely. She had begun bucking people off and snapping for no reason. As soon as I stood next to the mare, the whole left-hand side of my body began to ache. I felt extreme pain, almost to the point where I wanted to sit down and cry. My left leg felt tight and very sore. I was fine before I saw this mare, so I could only conclude that the pain I was feeling was a reflection of how the mare was feeling. I asked the owners if she had been involved in any accidents and they said that, the week before, she had slipped over onto her left-hand side whilst walking down a horse lorry ramp. She got up very quickly, looking unharmed, so they had assumed she was OK. The feelings I was getting enabled me to convince her owners that she needed medical attention urgently, and a trapped nerve on her left-hand side was indeed diagnosed and treated.

4. Voice

This is, without doubt, the most incredible connection of the four. When you hear voice you are not hearing the animals directly: you are hearing words and personality being translated through your own inner voice. In other words, you are still able to pick up accents (yes, some animals have accents!), or you may hear the odd foreign word. No matter where the animal is from in the world, you will hear the words coming through as English if you are English, or German if you are German, and so on.

A typical example of this occurred when I was in France many years ago. It was a hot summer's day and I was relaxing by the pool when I heard a tiny little elf-like voice say '*Bonjour*'. I looked around, but could only see another empty sunbed, a couple of empty chairs and the pool, where the water was still. There was no one else at the villa apart from me. Or so I thought.

'Hello? Anyone here?' I asked.

'*Bonjour*' went the little voice again.

I sat up and took my sunglasses off so I could get a good look around, but could see no one. Beginning to think I was hearing things, I took a big sip of my iced tea and settled back down to sunbathe.

'Hey, you . . . I said *bonjour!*' the little voice insisted.

This time I was aware of something under a bush to my right. As I looked closer a small dark nose appeared, with whiskers twitching. 'Aghh!' I yelped, realising what was staring at me. It was a huge brown rat! I quickly gathered my legs up beneath me and wrapped my sun towel tight around my body for protection.

'Go away! Shoo!' I tried to usher the creature away, but he just sat staring at me with a look of ridicule at my fear, as if waiting for me to calm down. Then he slowly walked from the edge of the bush onto the stone step by the poolside, his little face still staring right at me.

'What do you want?' I quivered.

'Wouldn't mind your *tasse de thé*.'

My what?, I thought, frozen to the sunbed in fright. The rat stuck his nose in the air and wriggled his whiskers as if he was smelling something. With a little scurry, which sent shivers through my body, he ran up to my cup of iced tea which was on the ground by my sunbed and began lapping it up happily.

I couldn't move. Nowadays rats don't scare me at all but, back then, I was terrified – first, because it was about the size of a giant guinea pig and, secondly, the pesky creature was talking (though I don't know why I was surprised at this).

He took his fill of tea, looked at me and said, '*Au revoir*,' and scuttled off with not even a thank you! I did notice however that he said only a few words in French and the rest in English. I can't explain this. In all my communications with foreign animals it seems that the words come through in English apart from the odd ones. I have never yet had a conversation where the animal spoke a totally different language. I must be somehow subconsciously translating them, maybe it's yet to happen to me, who knows? Other communicators also seem to experience voice in the same format as me. I am sure this is something I will be investigating in the future.

These four straightforward ways of communicating are the basis of all communication with animals. In my opinion, this is something that everyone has the ability to achieve. It just takes a little practice to open up your psychic ability, but once you do, the voice, pictures, video and emotions will begin to flood in and before you realise it, you too will be communicating with animals!

Chapter Eight

Although my job for the pet food company was OK, I didn't enjoy the constant travelling and being stuck in endless traffic jams. And I found the sales targets unachievable. I wasn't much good at it because my head and heart were elsewhere. I always knew I would have a career with animals; I just didn't know exactly how.

I wanted to use my psychic gift with the animals and I remembered reading a book about asking the universe for what you wanted, using something called cosmic ordering. I had never tried this, but I decided to give it a go. I sat down one afternoon with a plain piece of paper and wrote down what I wished for in the future. Happiness and health came first on my list, along with a great relationship and a wonderful life. At the bottom of my list I wrote: I want to talk with the animals, and work with them. I folded the piece of paper, held it over an ashtray and lit the corners with a match. I let it burn until all that remained were some cinders in the bottom of the glass ashtray.

A few weeks later, I was listening to Radio 2 as I drove home from work. They had a lady coming on to talk about animals, and I remember thinking she would probably be a dog trainer or something similar. But when this lady started talking she spoke about a skill called animal communication. She was describing inter-species communication: animals and humans talking to each other. I stopped my car and was transfixed by the sounds coming out of the radio. This woman was claiming she could talk to animals. The show was breathtaking. Then, right in the middle of the interview, my phone rang and cut the radio off. By the time I could get back to it, the interview was over.

I just couldn't get it out of my mind. Did that woman actually say she could talk with the animals? Was she doing the same as I had done? Was it a similar type of connection? I had a million questions running through my mind and no way of getting answers. I could not believe the phone had rung at the crucial part of the interview. I was gutted! I called a couple of friends to see if they had been listening, but no one had. Maybe I would never get my answers.

Later that week I was browsing the internet when I had an extreme urge to go to a spiritualist church. I hadn't been to one for a long time, but it was something I was suddenly keen to do, maybe because like-minded people would be there, people who believed in spirit. A friend and I found one for that evening and headed off. It was a busy night at the church and we were running late, so we were the last to get seats. 'Ow!' I yelped as I sat down. Lifting the culprit off the chair, I found a rolled-up newspaper called *The Psychic News*. My eyes locked onto the front page: there was the name of the lady who had been on the radio – and she was holding a workshop about five minutes from my house the following weekend.

I do believe in fate and psychic forces, but this was incredible. It was surely a sign. I booked on the course immediately.

I was told to turn up at ten on the Saturday morning and did so to the minute, as requested. I wasn't even sure what the day was all about. I just knew I had to be there. The weather was a little cloudy but dry, but to be honest there could have been thunderstorms and it wouldn't have bothered me. I was exactly where I wanted to be.

The course was being held at a local hotel south of Glasgow. We were greeted at the door by a lovely lady named Lorraine, who took our names and showed us to our seats. We sat in rows, waiting for the animal woman to come in. There must have been about thirty people there that day, some wearing smart dresses and others casually dressed in jeans and t-shirts. All of them had a notepad with them and most had photos in their hands. Some people looked really excited, others seemed embarrassed to be there and sat at the back with their heads down so as not to be noticed. A few were doing exactly what I was doing – having a good old nosy around the room. It was a pleasant function room. The seats were soft, the decor was neutral and it had huge glass doors that opened up to a large car park.

Suddenly I noticed Lorraine rush to one side and flick a switch on the music centre near the bar. She began clapping in rhythm and everyone joined in. The music changed to a loud samba tune, and in walked a flamboyant American lady. She was captivating, with a huge smile, and something told me she had hidden depths that I could only guess at.

She began to speak about who she was and what she did, and I felt really nervous sitting there listening to everything she had to say. I just did not know what to expect next. What if we got tested? Would I be able to deliver? I looked to my left and saw a girl of about nineteen, wearing a blue cardigan, and noticed she had a tear in her eye. I offered her a tissue and she gave me a nodding look of gratitude. Was she feeling the way I felt? Did she understand it all? Could she too speak with animals? I looked to my right to see a row of other attendees gazing up at the American lady, hanging onto her every word. Wow! This day was going to be mind-blowing.

I was not wrong. Before long we were working with live animals: first a dog, then a cat, and then, to my amazement, a horse in the car park. We were required to ask the animals questions, such as: What is your favourite food? What colour is your bed? Who do you live with? When we felt we had received the answers we wrote them down on our notepads. At the end of the exercise we each had to read out our answers to the rest of the group, with the animals' owners validating any correct information received. Most people got some of the questions right; I and another lady were getting almost every answer right: the owners were nodding, 'Yes, that's correct,' and looking slightly surprised that we were getting so much key information. I couldn't help but think that since these owners had brought their animals to the workshop, they must be prepared to hear what their animal has to say. I realised that some people use their communication ability more frequently than others, and just like a muscle, the more you use it the stronger it gets.

What a wonderful day I was having! After lunch we started to work with the photographs we had been asked to bring of an animal that we knew well. I took along a picture of Billy, my childhood pony. We shared our photos around among ourselves and began to read them, just as if the animals were standing in front of us in the flesh. To my surprise, people were gasping and some were even crying. I was one of them. Not only could I easily read a photograph the same way I was reading live animals, but other people could too. Everyone in the group was staggered, and so were the owners of the animal guests. The atmosphere in the room was electric.

I was in a state of total euphoria during the workshop. That was the day the light bulb in my head went on. What I was doing with the animals was perfectly natural, and I was not the only one who could do this:

there were other people out there, so I wasn't mad after all. At last I had found my calling. I knew this was what my future was going to be. I was going to turn my natural ability into my business. I was going to become an animal communicator, otherwise known as a pet psychic.

After the day was over I can only describe myself as an emotional wreck. I had to stop the car halfway home. It sounds silly, but I just sat and cried. All the frustration, the years of being doubted and of doubting myself had come to an end. By following my heart, I had unlocked my future. It was so clear.

When I finally arrived home my face was red and swollen due to the tears. Fraser was shocked to see me in such an emotional state. When I left that morning I had been looking forward to the course so much, and he wondered what on earth had happened.

I managed to blurt it all out to him and I think he was still slightly confused, but relieved I'd finally managed to understand what I could do.

For two whole days I cried. It was an emotional release that needed to happen before I could move forward with my life. From that moment on, my world changed. I resigned from my job and became a full-time professional animal communicator. It was me, it was real and it was just perfect.

Now I had to find customers. I decided the best way to make a start was to offer free readings. I placed a couple of simple adverts on the auction sites like ebay, thinking I would only get a few replies, and was shocked to find about forty people asking for a free reading. I spent the next few weeks practising, writing down on my notepad all the information I was receiving from the animals and surprising owners with the answers to their questions. And I turned one of the rooms in my house into a small office. I painted it a cool shade of blue, hung up a few pictures of my animals and bought a nice white desk for my computer. After that I was ready: ready to turn truly professional.

I was thrilled that I had finally found my feet. Word of mouth was working wonders. People from all over the UK started to contact me by phone and email for readings. All I needed to read for them was a clear photograph of their animal, alive or passed. Work was coming in quickly, and my readings were getting better. Now my daily life consisted of checking the post and working on that day's animal photos. I'd write all the information on some nice white paper and pop it into a large white envelope with the photograph and a business card I had had made up. I visited a few customers with their animals, but to be honest it is much easier to do a reading from a photograph. And I could truly say I was using my psychic ability.

For me, achieving a connection with the animals begins with being relaxed. If I am stressed about something, there is no way I can connect with another: there is no room for anything else. So relaxation is key. I believe our brainwaves are much faster than those of animals, and when we slow down, so too does our brain. By making a love link, we are able to get on the same level as an animal and achieve point of contact. This ability gets stronger and easier with practice.

One of my aims is to teach others how to communicate with animals, so I wrote a practical PowerPoint presentation to show the basics of giving a reading. After practising my speech I set up a one-day workshop in my own town, just like the one I had attended. It was a huge success and before long I was doing about three a month, scattered all around the UK. The people attending were having so much success – it was mind-blowing. It truly was fantastic.

I believe that even a sceptic can become a believer and I have proved this many times over the years, in workshops and in readings. One reading I did was for a client called Puffin, whose owner was a real sceptic. Unfortunately for Puffin's owner, his friend Jenny dragged him along to see me when I was doing one of my workshops. They both brought their animals for me to work with on the day, and this is when I met Puffin, a huge leopard-print giant of a cat. He was wonderful! All the students enjoyed working with the two animals and the information was coming in thick and fast. But I could see that Puffin's owner at the back of the room was not impressed.

'Are you hearing what your cat is telling us?' I asked.

'Well, yes, but you could have guessed all the infor-mation,' he grinned.

I knew he was still sceptical and I would have to get Puffin to help me. So I asked Puffin if he could tell me something only his owner would know – a secret, perhaps? (Cats are always great at telling us secrets!)

Puffin started to describe how his owner had got really drunk one night and forgotten to feed him. He sent me a picture in my mind of his owner collapsed in a drunken state in a huge armchair, can of beer in one hand and hamburger in the other. Puffin waited patiently for his dinner, but his owner fell asleep, having taken no notice of his calls for food. Hungry and a bit annoyed, Puffin decided he would go for a little holiday, thinking that this would make his owner take notice of him. So he slept in a neighbour's shed for two nights, catching his own food. His owner eventually found him, after a lot of panic, and greeted his return with a huge bowl of food.

When I revealed this information to Puffin's owner, his face went beetroot. Everyone thought it was really funny that Puffin had snitched on him, and I could see he was embarrassed but luckily he could see the funny side too. He confirmed that he had taken a little too much to drink that night and had forgotten to feed Puffin. He also confirmed that Puffin had gone missing, and that he had searched everywhere for him. He found him two days later, in the Wendy house next door. Puffin got a huge hug of appreciation and, best of all, the sceptic was no longer a sceptic.

Everything was going well but my excitement soon hit a huge problem that tested me, tested Fraser and tested our relationship. Although I could at last say, 'Yeeha!

It's real,' Fraser still couldn't totally accept it. I had spoken to him in the past about what I was doing, but I have noticed that men often hear what you are saying but do not always listen properly, so I think he didn't really understand the details at the beginning. Of course Fraser believed, without a shadow of doubt, that I had some sort of psychic ability. But he found it extremely hard to grasp that I was actually talking with animals.

Fraser has been a sceptic from the beginning. Most of us have been brought up with the belief that speaking to animals is impossible, so it is slightly worrying to be confronted with a fiancée who says she can do this. He knew all about my so-called psychic powers, and had seen the evidence with his own eyes, but it was my proof, not his.

So when I asked the famous question, 'Do you believe people can speak to animals?', he replied, 'No.' And I instantly took offence. If he didn't believe what I was doing was really possible, then he didn't believe I was telling the truth. How could he possibly think I was lying? I was heartbroken. My closest person, the one person that I trusted and thought trusted me, was basically saying I was a fake! It was a rough road to travel.

It got worse when we went out socialising. Friends would ask me what I was doing now and I would gush with excitement about my future as an animal communicator. But then they would turn to Fraser with a slight smirk and ask, 'Do you believe in this?' And he'd say, 'No, but I believe that Joanne can do it.' This didn't make sense to me. I felt embarrassed and betrayed that he couldn't support my belief, and it hurt. I felt so alone. Our relationship was already under a lot of strain at the time, and we suddenly became disconnected.

We talked and talked. As I realised what Fraser thought, it began to make sense. He had always grown up with animals, and he knew that all of them have their own personalities. He also knew that it was possible to become accustomed to each individual character and to have a connection with them through understanding them. But what he couldn't get his head around was that I could take it a step further and send and receive information. It took quite some time for Fraser and myself to get our relationship back on track, and boy am I glad we did. We never gave up.

I could write all day about some of the animals I have worked with. They are all amazing. So I would like to share some of my most memorable readings with you.

One was with a beautiful cat, a deep blue-grey British shorthair with stunning large yellow eyes. It was a slightly worrying reading, as he was a little poorly and had been seeing the vet. (I stress to all my clients that although I will help if I can, they must always see a vet first: I am not here to take a vet's job.) His owner wanted to know whether there was anything else she could do to help him.

Speaking with this cat, I got a connection straight-away. He kept saying over and over, 'Linseed oil, linseed oil – I need linseed oil.' I'd never heard of linseed oil being fed to a cat, and I wasn't sure whether they could eat it. I did get other information that the owner validated. But at the end of the reading I remembered what he had said and offered it to his owner. 'Just one last thing – he has told me he needs linseed oil.'

The phone went silent, and then his owner said, in a slightly shocked voice, 'Joanne, he has just this morning been diagnosed with an allergy to fish oils, and the vet has told me I must find a cat food that only contains linseed oil.'

The cat's information was right. He had not known the diagnosis, because he was outside when his owner took the vet's call. This little piece of information validated the whole reading for her. And after she found him a special cat food containing linseed oil, he became well again. A happy cat indeed.

One of my early readings was among the most difficult and thought-provoking that I have ever done. It really made me question what to do for the best.

The reading was of a dog. The owner was not worried about her dog, and there was no particular reason for the reading other than to be sure that the dog was happy. I was excited about reading her. The picture showed a rusty brown terrier, with a huge wet black nose. Her eyes were sweet-looking, but I could see something was worrying her.

I did the reading, all of which was validated by her owner, but I made the decision to withhold a piece of information the dog had shown me. Why? Because I felt the owner wanted and maybe needed to know her dog knew how much she loved her, and also how much the dog loved her owner. My job was to relay what the dog required. The dog knew what was happening and did not want me to tell her everything; I saw it as my place only to pass on what was intended. And so that's what I did. I asked the dog's owner to spend more time with her dog, and said it was important. She agreed and never questioned it.

The information I kept back was clear. I saw a picture of a man digging a garden, but when I looked more closely, I saw he was digging a grave, a dog-sized grave. And there above it was a large number 11. For some reason I just could not piece the information together, but I knew the dog was showing me the picture in my mind for a reason.

To my amazement, the dog's owner phoned me a couple of weeks after the reading. She was so upset, but when she could finally speak through her tears, she began to thank me for giving the two of them time together. I didn't understand what she was saying until she explained that, exactly eleven days after the reading, her dog had collapsed and died of a brain tumour. They buried her in their garden, just as I had seen in my mind! I never did tell the dog's owner what I saw, but I was happy they had spent their final days together.

I did wonder how the dog knew what was going to happen. I also wondered whether, if animals can talk whilst they are alive, they can also talk after their death. My questions were soon answered: I do believe the universe gives you answers exactly when you are ready for them.

Sometimes I have to be a pet detective as well as a pet psychic and this time was no exception.

I received a call from a very concerned owner of a little blue budgie called Davie.

The lady had come in from work and noticed her back window had been forced open. When she went into her house, it soon became clear that she had been burgled. She called the police and began to go through what was missing, only to discover that Davie and his cage had gone too. She couldn't understand what a burglar would want with her budgie, and prayed that the culprit would bring him back. She placed posters offering a reward in local shops, but no one had any information. She had almost given up hope, until she spoke to a friend who had heard of my work, and decided to give me a call. I explained to her that I would use my tracking technique and see what information I could get.

I was able to tune into little Davie quite easily, and at least he was alive and well.

'Davie, where are you?' I asked him.

'In the fire room,' he replied.

'Fire room? What do you mean?' I asked, a little confused.

'Fire room. Big fire and big dog,' he said, quite matter of fact.

This was going to be difficult. He just wasn't making sense to me.

'Is there anything you can see other than the fire and the dog?' I asked him.

'There is a tree.'

'What – in the house?' I asked.

'Yes,' he replied.

'Can you see outside? What can you see?'

'I see red children.'

Well, at this point I was really perplexed. Red children, a tree, a fire and a dog? I couldn't work out where he was from this information, so I had to dig a little deeper with my questioning.

'Can you tell me what the person who took you looks like?'

'Yes. He has me on his arm,' he replied.

'You? On his arm?'

'Looks like me,' he said.

So now I had red children, at tree, a fire, a dog and a budgie on his arm. Crikey! This was hard work.

'Do you know the person?' I asked.

'Yes,' he said.

OK, now we were getting somewhere. I rang his owner up and gave her the clues.

'I know who this is, Joanne,' she said. 'It's my cousin. He has an open fire, a pit bull terrier and a tattoo of a bird – not a budgie – on his arm that is the same colour as Davie.'

'That still doesn't explain the red children,' I said.

'Ah, well, it makes total sense. You see, opposite his house is a school and all the children have a red uniform.'

She was desperate to get off the phone and go and confirm the information. And she was right. The cousin had broken into her home to get money for drugs.

Knowing how much she loved Davie, he had kidnapped him, intending to hold him to ransom.

The police were called and Davie and some jewellery were both returned to their rightful home, much to the owner's relief. The cousin had been in jail for theft before and was eventually sent back there, and Davie had survived his big adventure unharmed.

My work was becoming more and more interesting. I was reading lots of animals, with many different stories. Some had passed, some were living, and others were in trouble, like Bobby, the missing kitty.

One Tuesday morning my phone rang. At the other end of the telephone line was a lady who sounded frantic.

'What on earth is wrong?' I asked.

'Oh, Joanne, I desperately need your help,' she replied, almost in tears.

'Of course. What's the problem?' I enquired.

She began to explain that she and her husband lived on a houseboat with their cats, Bobby and Betty.

Everything had been wonderful and their lifestyle was near-perfect. The cats enjoyed their life, moving slowly up and down the canals in the south of England, and never ventured off the boat. They were house cats – well, boat cats! One night, the family moored the boat up, due to heavy thunderstorms. The wind was howling and the lightning was striking an electrical display in the sky above. They settled down for the night but when they woke in the morning, Bobby had gone. He was nowhere to be seen. They checked every part of the boat, over and over, but found nothing. His owners were heartbroken. Bobby was only three years old and didn't know what life was like on dry land.

The worst of the news was that they had only moored for the night because of the bad weather, and they had to move the boat early in the morning to an official mooring site further up the canal. This was two miles from where they had originally stopped.

'We had to leave him!' she cried. 'He won't know where we are.' She was devastated.

'It's OK. Let me tune in and see what I can get for you.'

I have to say I didn't hold out much hope. Would

he be able to survive in the big wide world? I promised I would take a look at his photograph and see what information I could get, but warned that it might be difficult due to the circumstances of the weather conditions, the unknown area, and so on.

Settling down to work, I tried to make contact with Bobby. The initial connect happened quite quickly. However, I lost contact within minutes. What on earth was going on? Was he ill? Frightened? In danger? I had to get back to him as soon as I could. I tried again for the next hour and, finally, connection was achieved.

'Bobby, are you OK?' I asked anxiously.

'Yep, I'm busy. Come back later,' he replied.

Then he disconnected from me! I couldn't understand what was going on. This had never happened to me before. I was so worried about him. Later that day, I tried another connection, this time with success. I was delighted when he spoke to me.

'Can you speak now, Bobby? Why couldn't you talk earlier when I tried to talk to you?' I asked him.

'Yes, I'm fine. I was busy eating,' he replied quite calmly.

'Your owner is very worried about you. They have had to move the boat,' I explained.

'I'm fine,' he said again.

'Your mum will come and find you and take you home. Try and stay exactly where you are,' I said, and went on to ask him what he could see and smell so I could give his owner an idea of where he was.

But he interrupted me. 'No, tell her not to find me. I am fine. I will be back at four, before September, when things calm down. I am happy out here.' And with that he disconnected. It was the last time I managed to connect with him.

Feeling pretty down about the reading, I telephoned his owner to give her the news.

'Umm, it's not great news. I did get through but . . .'

'Oh my God! He's dead isn't he?' she said.

'No, no. Of course not,' I replied quickly. 'He's fine. In fact, he was quite matter of fact about it all. Bobby has asked you not to go looking for him.' Trust me, trying to tell anyone who has a missing pet not to go and look for them is not an easy task, but I had to be true to what I was receiving. 'He said he was fine, and that he would be back at four, before September.'

'But he doesn't know where we are,' she replied anxiously.

'All I can tell you is what he said to me, and that's

it, I'm afraid. But I trust he is OK. He said he would be back when things calm down a little.' I felt her dismay at what she was hearing, but there was nothing more I could offer. My worry was that she was right. I wondered how he would find his way home. They were several miles away from the place he went missing, and we were at the end of July. September was quite a long way off.

Weeks passed and then, out of the blue, the phone rang and I heard a familiar voice at the other end.

'Joanne, guess what?' the lady shouted down the phone.

'What? What's happened?'

'I heard a noise on the boat in the early hours of the morning, and when I went to investigate, there was Bobby. He was just sitting cleaning himself! He found us. Can you believe it? He really found us.' She was thrilled.

'That's fantastic news. I am so very pleased for you all. Just out of interest, what time did he appear?' I asked her.

'Umm, about 4am,' she replied.

'Can you remember, he said he would be back at four. And guess what? It's August the twenty-eighth, which means we are just before September!' We both laughed out loud.

I was so happy for them all and Bobby was none the worse for his adventure. As far as I'm aware he hasn't left the boat since. What a clever cat.

I still struggled with sceptics at that time, including a few in my extended family, a couple of friends from my old work and even some clients. I remember my nephew Ashlee saying to my mum that I had completely lost the plot and he found it embarrassing. I laughed it off but, secretly, knowing Ashlee thought of me as his mad auntie did hurt a little.

I continually felt the need to defend my work and my belief system. Eventually, as my self-esteem grew stronger, I realised that sceptics were just people who were still open to understand (well, most of them). So I set about inviting them on my workshops, answering their questions as best I could and showing how anyone could communicate if they just tried. Thankfully, the results were fantastic.

When he was finally ready (better late than

never!), Fraser decided he would like to see for himself what my workshops were all about. The workshop he came to was a busy one, and I think he was impressed that so many people wanted to hear this normal girl, his fiancée, talk about animal communication.

He sat, he watched, he learned, and he even joined in. I was thrilled. That day, he saw for the first time what I had been so excited about, and at last he understood. He even started reading books on the subject, so he could understand more about what I was doing and accept it. You could say I was running at 100 miles an hour, and he at 80. Fraser needed to learn for himself, in his own time, not as and when I wanted him to. Somehow, he has managed to catch up, and has gone from being a true sceptic to a scared believer. I say scared, because the whole psychic realm scares him. Fraser explains it as being afraid of the unknown, of not knowing what may happen next. He likes being in control of his world, but in the psychic realm something new and unexpected is happening all the time. I am so proud of him.

Chapter Nine

Our life together now consisted of animals, true love, and understanding. It was perfect. Toby, Klein and Mosko, our borzoi, were happy, but we decided to get another borzoi to keep Mosko company. Borzois (also known as Russian wolfhounds) are a beautiful and graceful breed. They were originally bred as sight hounds, so their natural instinct is to chase. The dogs have a minimum height of 29 inches and bitches 27 inches, and they have very long elegant heads with kind, almond-shaped dark eyes and neat ears, which lie close to the head. Their coats are of medium length, in any colour. Someone once described Mosko to me as a credit card with hair! I suppose they are similar to an Afghan hound, only much more elegant and aristocratic, in my opinion. They are very quiet and extremely sensitive, and such a pleasure to live with. They always demand your undivided attention, but resist that of strangers unless formally greeted – quite snobby, really.

At the time, I was really interested in showing. I wanted to go to the championship dog shows around the UK, where the most beautiful dogs, groomed to perfection, compete for type (the breed standard according to the UK Kennel Club), soundness and elegance. We had bought our first borzoi, Mosko, from a lovely lady called Sandra, and hoped he could compete at dog shows as well as being a pet. He was a bright tangerine and white dog, and very beautiful. However, Mosko had other ideas. He just wanted to be a pet. We knew this because he would always misbehave at the shows: not doing as he was told, holding his tail as high as he possibly could (when it should be kept low) and barking with excitement (borzois rarely bark). His funny antics at the shows convinced us he would prefer to stay as a pet. That was fine by us, as he is such a clown, and always makes everyone laugh.

One day we decided it would be fun for Mosko to go racing. After all, he is built for speed and, being a sight hound, should chase. Oh, how wrong we were! We all waited with bated breath, anticipating that this lean borzoi would undoubtedly be the leader of the race over the other dogs, who were mostly whippets and mongrels. The whistle blew and the lure, made of an old rag and a plastic bottle with fake fur attached to it, shot away from the start line. All the dogs leapt into action, bar one – Mosko. Instead, he thought it was hilarious, and proceeded to gallop and jump around the field, heading in the opposite direction to the rest of the dogs. Needless to say, we were never invited back! But he did become a bit of a celebrity later, being photographed in the *Pet Love* book of borzois, along with Klein and my new borzoi.

So, having had no success in the ring with Mosko, a show dog was my aim. After putting the word about for some days, a fellow exhibitor and friend suggested I contact a lady who was thinking about selling her two-year-old borzoi. She said he was a good dog and would teach me a lot. Perfect! I made the phone call and agreed to purchase him. We arranged to meet at the next show to discuss details and collect him. His name was Mozart, and I just knew he was going to be perfect for our family. What I didn't realise at that time was that Mozart would turn out to be one of the most important dogs in my life.

I was so excited as Fraser and I drove the long road to Leeds that morning. The show was held indoors in a type of sports hall. The place was mobbed with exhibitors and their beautiful borzois, all different colours and sizes from puppies to veterans. It really was a borzoi lover's heaven. We decided to go up and stand on the balcony where we would have a better view of the dogs and wait for Jean (Mozart's mum) to come in with him. Now, I know this sounds a little mad, but we had no idea what Mozart looked like. I had agreed a price and the collection without even seeing a picture of him. We knew what Jean looked like, but not Mozart. We waited, and waited. To pass the time, Fraser and I commented on the dogs as they walked in through the hall doors. None of them was quite right for us: either they were the wrong colour, shape or temperament. But then we both went completely silent as this huge, stunning dog glided in, his deep mahogany and white coat flowing and glimmering in the light.

'Wow! Now that's a borzoi!' Fraser gasped.

I could hardly breathe through sheer admiration of this dog below. 'Oh my God, he is spectacular!' I whispered. When we looked down he seemed to be the only dog in the room. We were awestruck. Then, to our amazement, Jean appeared, tottering in behind him.

'No way. You don't think . . .'

It was Mozart! We were both stunned.

Mozart came to live with us from that day, and the first few weeks were not easy. He missed Jean and just didn't want to be with us. He was grieving for the life he had known. It was heartbreaking to watch. He stared up at our garden fences, trying to find a way out, and he wouldn't come into the house at night but stayed outside in the garden shed. I made him a bed in there, and just hoped he would eventually come round. Mosko would try and play with him, but he wasn't interested. It was awful. He was struggling to comprehend why he had been taken away.

Fraser and I felt so guilty, and after a few weeks we came to a decision: if Mozart wasn't in the house by the weekend, accepting us as his new family, then we would take him back to his old home. We couldn't bear to see him suffer any more. I was so upset: he was my dream dog and Mosko loved his company. I decided to sit and talk to him. I didn't expect it to work, because he wouldn't connect with me. He averted his eyes whenever I was with him and I could never get his focus on me long enough to make a connection, but I had nothing to lose. I had to try.

And so I sat and explained why he was with us. I described the life he would have in our home and told him that he would see his mum Jean again, but that he would probably be sold on to someone else if he went back home – so it might be better to stay with us. I told him he would be loved and I promised that I'd take care of him for ever. It's always difficult talking with my own animals, because I already know them and so cannot validate the information I receive as I can with someone else's. I just have to trust that my words get through and that what I receive back is real.

That evening Fraser came home from work and said, 'Any change with Mozart?' Feeling pretty low about the situation, I said there wasn't and we would probably have to take him back that weekend. But the next day Mozart was a different dog. You see, no one had told him he was being sold, he had had no idea he was changing homes and so he had been confused and stressed. He had heard me all right and soon settled in. He became part of the family and Mosko's best friend. They played, ate and slept together.

We went to shows and did well. Mozart was a brilliant teacher and guided me quietly, showing me the best way to handle him and to make the most of his elegance. This dog actually did the showing himself. I was just the accessory on the end of the lead. He was fabulous.

I had a deep love connection with him, and knew it was mutual. But strangely enough there was no communication connection, at least not through words, pictures or videos. He was a strong silent type. Although he would stare deeply into my eyes, almost melting my heart with love, he would never actually communicate with me. I even took him to a communication workshop with another communicator and guess what? He said nothing. Not a dickybird.

When Fraser and I moved house we had a large kennel and run built for Mosko and Mozart. They loved the space, the fresh air and the freedom. When I went out to check and feed them, Mozart always, without fail, greeted me with a huge cheesy grin. He curled his lips away from his white teeth, grinning as hard as he could, and when someone smiles at me like that, I just cannot help but smile back. So every morning we greeted each other with a huge smile full of love. Wonderful! Mozart loved nothing more than to sit with his long nose over my shoulder and cuddle, all the while making a sighing noise as if totally content. He was so very affectionate, but very quiet indeed. All the time Mozart was with us, I only heard his voice once. But I felt emotion, deep emotion that melted my heart. He truly was a beautiful soul, and I loved him with all my being.

Soon our two borzois became four, with the arrival of our baby borzois, Rosie and Ruben. Ruben grew up to be a big red mahogany borzoi with a look about him of the cartoon character Snoopy, and had a temperament that was second to none. He was so special that he would probably have made a champion, but he never made the show ring due to a problem with his teeth. He passed unexpectedly of a kidney failure when he was only five. We will never forget him.

Rosie is a super dog, and a complete mummy's girl. Wherever I go, she goes too. Rosie has been my most successful show dog, gaining five Challenge Certificates and lots of other prizes. She is not only a proven Championship Show Champion, she is also my friend. I adore her and those who have been lucky enough to meet her over the years will agree how very special she is.

All my big dogs have had utter respect for Klein. Even though, size-wise, he's like an ant standing next to a horse, he always remains top dog. This gorgeous, precious, most amazing little tiger (OK, toy poodle) is one heck of a dog. Together we have had some hurdles in life to overcome, but he fights on, brave and strong. His nickname is 'Daddy's little tiger'. He may be small, but he is the boss. Klein is the love of my life. He is always with me, and our love for each other is unconditional. He even shares his love with Fraser, which I never thought would be possible, but the two of them have a unique understanding. Klein's favourite food is chicken, and although he would never communicate with me freely, he would soon pipe up with any information that I required if I offered him chicken.

For example, one morning my toothbrush disappeared. I just had a feeling Klein might know something about it. He always watched everything Fraser did and followed him around the house like a little shadow.

'OK, Klein,' I said, waving some chicken past his nose. 'Give me the answer, please. What's Daddy done with my toothbrush?'

'In his bag,' came the reply, as quick as lightning. It was a clear voice, steady and exact. It had no particular accent but there was a hint of warmth and personality.

'What bag?' I asked.

'Golf bag. It's in his golf bag.' And with that he gulped the piece of chicken I was holding and walked off.

Later that day, Fraser arrived home from his round of golf.

'Honey, have you seen my toothbrush?'

'No,' he replied.

'Really? Are you sure?' I quizzed.

'No, I haven't.'

'Well, Klein tells me you have it in your golf bag. Shall we see?' I laughed.

'Klein, you little snitch!'

And yes, there it was in his golf bag! Needless to say, I bought another toothbrush that day.

Mozart was two years old when he came to live with us, and the life expectancy for borzois is between nine and thirteen years, although one I know is still with my friend at the age of fourteen. Sadly, Mosko passed at the young age of five. He developed a disease that he could not fight, and we lost him. We will never forget his brightness, and the fun and laughter that he brought to our family. He and Mozart were best buddies and Mozart felt the grief really badly. He was upset for weeks, wouldn't eat or play, and just lay in his kennel, quiet and very sad. Even the pups we had at that time could not help him, although I am glad they were there to keep him company.

I truly felt his pain. There were no words, but the emotion was so strong. It was a deep emotional pain in my heart, a feeling of loss. I have noticed that people who are learning to communicate often feel the animal's emotions rather than hear clear voices; they do not realise where the emotions are coming from and so the animal's grief and feelings go ignored. By asking yourself why you are feeling these emotions and understanding that perhaps they aren't yours, but the feelings of the animal in question, you will be able to help them. This is why, when you are learning to communicate, you must learn to notice and analyse every slight change in your own emotions in order to understand what is happening with your animal.

Animals are so sensitive to our emotional needs and we often overlook theirs. They need us to understand them.

Early one Sunday morning I was called to see a beautiful chestnut pony called Mr Tibbs. He was as red as a carrot, chunky like a chip and full of character. His owner wanted to know why he had a strong dislike of the indoor school at their livery yard. Whenever he went anywhere near the school, he would put the brakes on and refuse to budge. Nothing would change his mind.

Mr Tibbs was very easy to talk to and connected with me almost instantly. In fact, I think he found it quite amusing. I began my conversation on a positive note, and said, 'Hi, Mr Tibbs! How are you today?'

'Hungry!' he replied. And he sent me a picture of a blue bucket, full to the brim with pony nuts. It was almost overflowing.

'Is that what you want? All those nuts?' I asked.

'Will you get them for me?' he said.

'No, I can't,' I laughed.

'Why not, lady? Please, get me the food,' he said, shaking his head and nearly knocking over his owner.

It was funny having a pony that looked a little on the podgy side demanding I get him food. I said, 'I am not here to get pony nuts. I'm here to ask you about the issue you have with the indoor school.'

'Get me the food and I will answer your questions,' he replied.

This was the first time I had come across an animal who was willing to be bribed to share information – apart from my poodle Klein, who would always talk for a piece of succulent cooked chicken. But this was different: Mr Tibbs was so demanding! I turned to his owner and explained that he wouldn't answer my questions unless he had some pony nuts. She laughed, and told me how greedy was. Apparently it was a standard joke on the yard, and they had given him the nickname Porky. He would never do anything without a food bribe – he would probably have walked over crocodiles for pony nuts if he had to. The only time it didn't work was when she tried to take him into the indoor school.

Mr Tibbs gulped down the pony nuts on offer like he'd never been fed before.

'OK, will you talk to me now?' I asked.

'Yep. What do you want to know?' he said.

'Why won't you go into the big barn?' I asked, thinking it was a safe bet to call it a big barn rather than an indoor school.

'I'm never going in the circus. Never!' he snapped.

'Circus? What circus?' I said, confused.

'Your pony is talking about a circus,' I told the owner. 'Do you understand what this means?'

'No, I have no idea what he is going on about,' she replied.

So I went back with more questions. 'Tell me about the circus. What was it like?'

'I was scared. I saw a man hit my friend and she fell over.' He started to fidget. I could see he was feeling anxious about his memory.

'It's OK, Mr Tibbs. You are safe now. Who was the man?' I asked him.

'I don't know. He was taking them into the circus.'

'What is a circus, Mr Tibbs?' I thought this might explain where he was at the time. I couldn't help but wonder why a circus would want a fat, carrot-coloured pony and his friend: the horses I had last seen at a circus were huge grey Lipizzaner stallions.

'The man called it a bloody circus,' he said, tossing his head in the air.

'Did you go into the circus, Mr Tibbs?' I asked.

'I was turned away at the door. Someone put me on a lorry and that was all I saw. I miss my friend,' he replied.

'But what did you see?' I insisted.

'Lots of people, a round area, lots of shouting and a man hitting my friend,' he began. 'It was the same as the big barn, and I am not going in there. They will beat me!' He swung his neck round and pulled his owner towards the stable.

I'd got it! I knew what he was talking about. I walked over to the stable where Mr Tibbs and his owner had repositioned themselves.

'Where did you get Mr Tibbs? Was it at a horse sale?' I asked his owner.

'Yes,' she answered. She had bought Mr Tibbs from a sale but she had done a deal with his previous owner and so he hadn't gone into the saleroom.

I asked her if she could tell me what the saleroom looked like.

'It was inside a barn.' She looked at me and her jaw dropped. 'It looked like our indoor school.'

'Mr Tibbs,' I said, 'it wasn't a circus. You were at a horse sale.' What Mr Tibbs had experienced was a horse sale with a circular indoor pen where horses are paraded for potential buyers. Sometimes they use sticks to move the horses. I can't be sure, but I suspect that is what he had seen when he said a man was hitting his friend.

We had solved the problem. Mr Tibbs thought the indoor school was another horse sale. He was scared and didn't want to go in, no matter what. So I explained that it wasn't a circus or a sale, and that it was just a nice place to go. It would be quiet and peaceful, and there would be no people there with them other than the odd groom. I explained that he would be safe and, with his owner's permission, told him he would be with her for life.

Mr Tibbs must have taken in all this information because, when I spoke to his owner a couple of days later, she told me that he had hesitated a little, but then walked into the indoor school, for the first time ever. And the other great news was that his friend at the sale, a little black and white pony, had been traced and was stabled only a few miles up the road. Mr Tibbs' owner had arranged for them to meet up again so he could see for himself that his friend was safe. Happy ending for Mr Tibbs!

People assume they have done enough for the animals, but one of the reasons why I feel communication is so very important is that it has taught me to listen. Sometimes we are just not aware of what they are feeling, or why. Animals are capable of incredible sensitivity, and they pick up on our emotions, feelings and loneliness.

One cold winter's evening in early November, I was driving back from a workshop in the Midlands. I was only about a hundred miles away from my home when I heard a loud bang and my steering veered to the left. I had driven over something sharp on the road and punctured my front tyre. This was my second puncture in two weeks, so you can imagine how annoyed I was. Pulling into a service station, I called for help on my mobile phone and the lady at the RAC reassured me that I would be towed all the way back home by a recovery vehicle. Relieved, I sat and waited for my knight in shining armour to come and rescue me.

After a short while the recovery vehicle arrived, and out jumped a large, jolly-looking man, who proceeded to attach my car to the back of the truck. I signed the paperwork and confirmed my destination.

'Jump in, and get warm,' he said, pointing to the cab.

'Great. Thanks,' I replied, heading swiftly towards the door. By now I was freezing my socks off!

'Oh, you don't mind dogs do you?' he said.

If only he knew where I had been and what I had been doing. Contrary to popular belief, I only tell people if they ask. I chuckled to myself and replied, 'Dogs? No, not at all. I'm perfectly fine with dogs.'

'Well, make yourself comfortable then. She doesn't bite,' he said, good-humouredly.

Staring through the window of the cab was a little Border terrier. She was as black as coal. (I know – Borders are meant to be a rusty brown colour. She must have been working with her owner in a garage.)

'Her name's Baby,' he called to me from behind the cab.

I opened the door, and she greeted me with her little wagging bottom.

'Hey, Baby! You are gorgeous, aren't you?' I smiled, trying not to get covered in the dirt she was wearing.

And at that point of contact, it happened. I suddenly had an overwhelming sense of emotion, a feeling of deep loss, of awful grief. There was absolutely no doubt in my mind that this little dog had lost someone close to her. My stomach began to feel uneasy. I actually felt quite sick, and the colour drained from my face.

'You poor thing,' I whispered to her. 'Have you lost someone?'

Just as I asked the question her owner jumped into the cab. I do not blurt out to anyone that I can talk to animals, so I decided to keep quiet and send the little dog some healing and love. But I was in no doubt of her loss. I could feel it. She was communicating through emotion.

We headed off on our journey and the little dog sat on my lap, accepting the healing and comfort that I offered to her. I couldn't help but feel she was soaking up my female energy, which led me to assume she was missing her human mum. What was it about the feeling I was getting? It was so strong. It touched my heart. Why would this dog make me feel so poorly? Hoping to get some answers, I struck up a conversation with her owner.

'You are very lucky to have such a wonderful little dog,' I said, smiling at him.

'Yes, she's a good girl. Comes to work with me now, since . . .' And then he stopped. I could see he was holding back his feelings.

'It's OK. You have both lost someone very close, haven't you?'

He turned and looked at Baby, as if she would give him courage to speak to me.

'My wife. Baby was her dog. I bought her as a Christmas present when she was poorly, so that when I was out at work and couldn't be there for her, Baby could keep her company until I came home.'

I just knew what was coming next. I felt it in the pit of my stomach.

'She died two months ago. She had cancer,' he began, and then told me how they had been married for over twelve years, very happily. His wife had felt a little unwell and popped down to her doctor's for tests, to be told she had cancer, and only had months to live. He took several weeks off work because she was feeling unwell, and one morning they went to the hospital for a check-up, but she never returned home. She collapsed and died in the waiting room. 'Baby never leaves my side now,' he explained, holding back the tears.

It all made sense. Baby had been sending me the feelings and emotions to show me what her human mum had been going through. I was feeling some of the effects of cancer.

My heart went out to her owner. How hard it must have been to tell me his story, and how much he and

Baby relied on one another for love and support. They needed each other and had a common bond with his wife.

The sickness I felt had gone, my colour returned and I began to feel fine again. Maybe they just needed to talk to someone. Maybe that person was me. I will never forget that night, or those two. I would like to think it was a little bit of emotional release for them both. And they could move on with life together.

One day I received a call from a lady whose dog William had disappeared that morning. She was really upset as her dog was fifteen years old and had never been away from her before. Her husband and the dog had gone for their usual walk to fetch the paper from a local shop. As the pair walked across the field opposite their house, William suddenly ran off. The husband searched the field but had no luck, so he returned home, thinking that William might have headed back there. When he got to the house, William was nowhere to be seen. The husband and wife looked everywhere, but no one had seen him. Finally, she called me, having heard about my work tracking missing animals. She explained that his behaviour was completely out of character. He had crossed the same field every morning for fifteen years and had never run off before. They emailed the photo of William over to me straightaway and I began tuning in. I was not prepared for what I saw.

In my mind I could see William walking across the field with his owner, and then I saw him suddenly run across the field with determination. I followed him in my mind as he went far away from his owner and saw him run out onto a main street and, to my horror, straight between two cars. He was hit by a pick-up truck. I couldn't believe what I was seeing! It was horrible. The pick-up truck screeched to a stop and a young man jumped out. He picked the dog up and placed him on the rear seat of the pick-up.

At this point William was still alive. The young man was not from the area and drove away in a hurry to get the dog to safety. I could see it all in my mind like a video. All of a sudden I had a deep sense of William passing to spirit on the back seat of the pick-up. He was gone.

'William, can you hear me? I'm Joanne. Will you talk to me?' I asked, and he connected straightaway.

'William, what has happened to you? Why did you run away?'

He told me that he had overheard his human mum saying she was really concerned about him. She was worried that his health was failing and she wouldn't be able to cope if she had to put him to sleep.

'So I thought I'd do it for her,' he said.

'What?' I was shocked at what I was hearing.

'Well, she said she wouldn't be able to cope, so I did it for her,' he explained. 'Tell her I love her.'

In my experience, animals do not see death as we do. They just move to another place, no big deal. Life goes on for them. Once William knew he didn't have long to live he decided he would pass on his own so his owner wouldn't have to make the decision for him. He got himself run over on purpose.

I sent him all my love and promised I would pass the message on to his owner. It was one of the most difficult situations I had found myself in, and I wasn't sure how to tell his human mum.

I phoned her and said, 'Did you talk about William passing to the spirit world recently? And did you say you wouldn't be able to cope making a decision to help him?' I was hoping she would agree.

'Yes, just two days ago. I was talking to my sister about it. Why?' she asked.

'Oh, I know what's happened to William.'

I was dreading telling her what I had seen. I explained that I could be wrong, and I hoped he would turn up at her door at any time, but I could tell her the information I had seen and heard, if she wanted me to. She said she did, so I explained what William had heard her say and what he had shown me. It was a sad day, but she thanked me for the information and set about trying to find out what had happened to his body.

A couple of days later, she called me back with an update. They had got a call from the young man after he asked around the village for the owners of a dog that he had described. He confirmed sadly what had happened to William and showed them where he had buried him, as he couldn't find out who he belonged to at the time. I suppose it was a little easier for William's owner to accept, as she had already heard about it from me via William. And because she now knew my information was correct, she was sure William lived on in spirit. This was a great comfort to her and her husband.

Animals can feel physical pain, just as we do. And sometimes the pain they feel is emotional.

I read a horse called Maizie, a beautiful patchwork mare, black and white in colour (the official term is piebald). Maizie's owner was a complete novice but, luckily for Maizie, she fell instantly in love with her the moment their eyes met. She went with her gut feeling and her heart (always the best way) when she purchased her, not really knowing what she had bought. Now Maizie's owner was really worried about her because she seemed extremely sad and depressed. She had also been diagnosed with a liver problem but she wasn't getting any better and the vet had almost given up hope.

My worst fears were realised when I tuned in. I instantly felt overwhelming sadness, as well as extreme anxiety and helplessness. Then a sudden feeling of grief overcame me, and the horse was showing me a video in my mind of what had happened to her. She showed me her previous home, where she had given birth to a foal. Maizie was a proud mother and loved her baby very much. The foal, barely weaned, was removed from her care and taken away. She never saw it again. Maizie was distraught. She was carrying this grief and loss, constantly reliving the moment when her foal was taken from her. She had lost the will to live. Maizie was in a desperate state and everyone at the owner's yard told her the horse was trouble, and it would be best to sell her as soon as possible. However, the love between them was too strong and, luckily for Maizie, her owner held firm and wasn't willing to give up.

I worked on the foal issue first, and we put Maizie in a field with a young horse. She knew it wasn't her foal, but she enjoyed her motherly role looking after the new filly. At the same time, I realised the liver damage was due to poisoning: no one had noticed that there were poisonous plants in her field. We now had a better understanding of what was wrong with Maizie. Once moved to a new field with her new buddy, Maizie soon picked up and before long was totally well again. The two horses became inseparable; Maizie accepted the loss of her foal, and looked after the filly like one of her own. The vet's treatment began to work its magic and now her health is great. Life looks perfect for Maizie.

I am so very pleased that Maizie's owner had the love connection with her and didn't pay attention to the advice from the people on the yard, even though they were more experienced horse owners. It is amazing what you can find by communicating with your animal, rather than giving up on it when its starts to misbehave.

One very lucky cat had been hanging around outside our home, living rough, for about a year and a half. She was a shabby little black and white moggy, with a ripped ear from some fight, and a turned-up nose. She fascinated me. I couldn't help but feel her pull towards me.

I put food out for her and welcomed her in, but she was scared of people and would never come near me. The closest I could get was about a hundred feet. I could feel her keeping an eye on me and if she saw me look at her, she would run for her life. She was closed off to all communication through fear, although I felt her wishing she could change.

Her name became Puss Puss, because that's what I called when putting out her food. I always fed her at night, so she could eat in peace, and I would go indoors and watch through the window blinds so she would not catch sight of me. Puss Puss slept through the coldest winters, rain, sleet or snow, warm inside one of the barns on the farm. I was never too worried about her. She had learnt to survive.

It is extremely hard to connect with feral animals that are scared of humans, and I assumed that I would have to accept her staying at a distance. Her mistrust of people just could not be overcome. But that changed one morning when my new baby Siamese Oshan decided to sneak out of the house to explore the great outdoors. Oshan is a house cat and we live on a busy main road, so this could have been a disaster – and I had no idea he had gone.

I suddenly noticed Puss Puss walking towards our house, which was obviously very odd. So I went and opened the back door slowly, knelt down and watched. She stopped in her tracks when she saw me.

'Puss Puss,' I called softly.

And to my astonishment she looked right into my eyes and walked straight up to me. This little cat, who had never looked at me once in a year and a half, was now sitting right in front of me, staring at my face. I couldn't help but feel she was trying to tell me something; so I thought, I've nothing to lose, I will ask her, not thinking that I would get an answer.

'Puss Puss, is there something you want to tell me?' I whispered gently, so as not to scare her.

'Yes. He's outside!' this little feminine high-pitched voice squeaked, sounding very worried.

'Who?' I asked.

'The kitten. The kitten is out,' she replied, still sounding anxious.

Oh, my gosh! I knew instantly what she meant. As soon as it registered in my heart that Oshan was outside, Puss Puss swiftly turned and ran into the back garden, with me following closely behind. She let out a huge meow, and there, under our lilac bush, was a very scared little kitten.

I was so grateful to her and offered her all my love and thanks. I also said she was welcome to come into the house and get warm any time. I was in no doubt that she had probably saved the life of my kitten that day, and she had had to overcome her own fears so she could open up and communicate with me, let alone come close. Her bravery was clear to see. She was determined to take care of another. I will be for ever grateful.

It did take a couple of days for her to feel safe enough to be stroked and handled, but eventually Puss Puss decided she could trust us and finally moved in. Today she has attached herself not to me, but to my partner Fraser. Wherever he is, she is not far away. It is easy to see how happy she has become. Her daily routine is to jump, skip and play outside, then come in for food and a long sleep. She brings us the odd live present now and then, and communication is essential whenever this happens. We thank her but explain that live mice and birds are not acceptable in our home.

Chapter Ten

As well as my communication with animals I saw an opportunity for a more holistic approach to them. I had started to deal more and more with animals suffering from fears, for example of going to the vet or to be groomed, and I decided to open the first grooming salon in Scotland that could really understand the animals and help them re-establish their confidence whilst being pampered and clipped. Any profession has both good and bad practitioners, but there are a lot of bad groomers out there, and only a handful who take a real interest in how the animals are feeling and treat them with respect. I opened the salon Pet Spa in central Scotland and it became an instant hit. The salon specialises in nervous and rescue animals who find new situations difficult to cope with or have suffered a bad experience that has filled them with fear. It is a place where the animals are looked after with dignity and respect. I work a couple of days in the salon at the moment, and the rest of the week I work from home, doing my readings. It's the perfect mix.

I see many animals coming through the salon doors. We have dogs and cats of all breeds and sizes coming in for their beauty treatments, such as bathing, blow drying and hair styling. Most enjoy being pampered and I only need to use my communication skills to reassure the new ones that they will be fine. Most of them settle after about five minutes with no problem.

However, some animals are more of a challenge. My salon manager Yvonne had been warned to expect the worst with one little dog who was coming to us for the first time. Her name was Milly and she had just been rescued from a puppy farm, but she wasn't a puppy – she was one of the breeding bitches. So prepared, we waited on Milly's arrival.

In walked a lovely lady, with a bedraggled skeleton covered in matted fur in her arms. If I hadn't seen a little nose poking out from beneath the fur I would never have known that the bundle was actually a dog. Her new owner was crying with relief as she handed her over to Yvonne.

The first step was to try and remove all her coat so the mats wouldn't harm her any more. They were so tight that she couldn't even walk, and she had very little strength or muscle even to try. As the clippers worked their way through the thickly matted coat, a tiny little black and white shih-tzu dog emerged from underneath. And what a sorry sight she was. In fact, I have never seen anything so bad in my eighteen years of working with animals. How could people be so cruel? It broke our hearts to see her in such a state. But our job was to make her feel better and I could feel her gratitude to us for what we were doing.

After she was fully clipped I took her to our bath to enjoy a nice warm soak. With her little body nuzzling into me, I began to place her down into the inch of warm water in the bath. I certainly did not expect what happened next: my communication kicked straight in and a sudden feeling of utter panic came over me. It caught me unawares as I was concentrating on getting her safely into the bath. I could hear screaming in my head. It was Milly, crying out in alarm. I scooped her frail little body back up into my arms. The path to communication was wide open and I began to feel overcome with fear. The fear was Milly's, not mine. My body was shaking all over as I raced Milly back to the grooming area.

'What the hell has happened?' said Yvonne, alarmed at the sight of us both shaking.

The communication between Milly and me was now coming in thick and fast. Milly suddenly started to show me pictures in my mind. It was horrific. As I held and comforted her, I saw Milly watching a man picking up each of her four puppies and placing them, one at a time, into a bucket of water. He waited until they stopped breathing before throwing them back down on the floor, and Milly was totally helpless to save them. She had watched each one of her babies being murdered.

The scene in my mind and the feeling in my heart for this poor little dog were overwhelming. Tears filled my eyes.

'Oh, Yvonne, it's the water. She thought I was going to drown her, just as her babies were drowned.'

This was one of those times when I've heard something so terrible from an animal, I almost wish I couldn't understand what I was being told. Happily, I was able to explain to Milly that I was not going to hurt her, and to tell her how sorry I was about what had happened to her. I focused on calming her down, sending her thoughts like everything is fine, and you are safe here. And I sent her pictures in my mind of her enjoying being bathed and groomed, visualising every stage for her, calm and relaxed. Eventually she allowed me to bath her and make her feel better. She was so brave. I will never forget the face of her owner when she came to collect her. The emotions took over and she cried all over again when she saw how different the little dog looked.

After explaining to Milly's owner what had happened, she told us that the breeder had been going to put her to sleep after she gave birth to four deformed puppies, which he had drowned. She had been over-bred, and she was no good to them if she couldn't produce healthy puppies. Now her ordeal was over and she had a lovely home where she could spend the rest of her life being loved. I will never forget her story.

Fraser and I now had the dogs and two cats, Oshan and Puss Puss, and we were soon to be joined by yet another. In my experience, even something simple such as giving an animal the right name is incredibly important. Animals can really become upset if we get it wrong, so it's always best to ask them. Take Chana, for instance.

I have always admired the Siamese breed of cat, and after getting Oshan I was really keen to get another. I saw a pure black Oriental cat at a local show one Saturday, and my mind was made up: that was the type and breed I was going to try and find. (Orientals are Siamese, but in solid colour.) It proved really hard. I must have spent two days phoning round every Siamese and Oriental breeder in the country. No one had a black Oriental. I was offered every other colour of cat, but not black.

My search was proving very difficult indeed, until I came across a friend of a friend who was a breeder based in Manchester. One of her show cats had just had a litter of kittens and among all the other colours was a tiny black Oriental girl. Her name was Rose, and as soon as I heard about her I knew she was meant to be with us. It would be thirteen weeks before she was ready to leave her mum, and the wait seemed to take for ever. Time goes extremely slowly when you are waiting for something special.

Meanwhile, I had a dilemma. My dog was called Rosie, and we didn't think it would be fair to have two Rosies at home, so the kitten would have to change her name. I find that animals are usually quite happy to change their name when moving to a new home. Sometimes the change can be really positive for them, especially if they previously had a stupid name, or they have suffered trauma. But in our case, it was just a simple case of twin identity.

The time came when the new name was to be chosen. Fraser asked if I had a name in mind, but I knew it wasn't my choice. I was going to let Rose pick her own name and this was a perfect opportunity to use my skill as an animal communicator. Rose's breeder had been very kind to us during the thirteen weeks and kept us updated with photographs of Rose's progress. So I sat with a photograph and tuned in. I explained to her that she would need a new name and asked if there was a name she would like to be called. Suddenly a little voice said something. I could barely make out what she was trying to say, but it sounded like China.

'China. That's nice. You want to be called China?' I said. I loved the name and was pleased she had chosen it. Let's face it, it could have been ghastly!

Again the little voice said China, or so I thought. But then it became a little clearer.

'No. It's Chana. My name is Chana,' she insisted.

'Chana?' I was taken aback. What did Chana mean? I had liked China, and had never heard the name Chana before. It was an odd name, but I thought I had better learn to accept it. And so her request to be called Chana was confirmed, and her show name became Mazpahs Chana Black. What I wasn't expecting was that Chana turned out to be a real name. Not only that, but it means graceful in Hebrew. It describes her to a tee.

I have tried to find out why she chose Chana. Did she know it was Hebrew? I don't know, because whenever I ask the question, the only answer I get is, 'It's my name, Chana', and nothing more. I can only deduce it is purely because she is graceful.

Eventually little Chana came home to us and settled in perfectly. She is doing brilliantly at the cat shows, too, winning almost everything. Oshan and Chana are now almost impossible to separate. All in all, choosing to have Chana come and live with us was one of the best decisions we ever made.

When animals come into my grooming salon, I know that, much as I adore them, especially the ones that are looking for new homes, I simply cannot take them home. I don't have the room for more. Or so I thought.

In came a lady carrying a basket containing a white Persian cat called Fluffy. We had been asked to clean him up and I lifted him out to examine his coat before his owner left. (This is something we always do at the salon, so we can explain to the owners what we will be doing whilst they are away.) Out came this white mass of mats, with huge orange eyes that looked right at me.

'Hello, gorgeous!' I said to him.

'Will you take me home?' piped up this voice.

I remember putting him down on the table and saying something like, 'Look, let's just get you feeling better.'

His owner left him in our capable hands, and Yvonne got to work on him. Boy, was he in a state. Every inch of the cat was matted deep down to the skin. He was such a good boy, and lay really still whilst we clipped away the mats.

'Will you take me home with you?' he said again.

'Yvonne, the cat wants to come home with me! He really does,' I said.

'Would you want to take him, really?' Yvonne laughed.

I picked him up so he was facing me. 'Do you really want to come home with me?' I asked.

'Yes,' he replied.

He was so gorgeous: pure white with a flat face and huge round orange eyes. He looked like an owl. This cat was absolutely nothing like the Siamese and Oriental breeds that I liked, but he had a beautiful energy that I was drawn to.

'Why on earth would the owner let you have him? He's a pedigree. She will never give him away,' Yvonne said.

When his owner came to collect him, I took a deep breath and said, trying not to sound too cheeky, 'If you ever need a home for Fluffy, I would gladly take him.' I waited for a response, expecting the worst.

'Really? That would be brilliant,' she replied.

Yvonne and I looked at each other in amazement.

She explained, 'It's just, I rescued him from a neighbour's house. We were caring for him with another short-coated cat while his elderly owner was in hospital.

Only, she just died. I took him in, but I can't keep him. He doesn't get on with my other cats.'

I looked at Fluffy and he looked straight back. I knew he wanted to be with me, and so the lady kissed him goodbye and I took Fluffy home. He settled in very quickly, almost as if he had always been with us. He likes toast in the morning and a cup of tea before bedtime. He adores his food. The only problem was that he wasn't responding to his name, so I asked if he would like to change it. And guess what he said? 'Call me Vegas.' What a great name! It suits him so much, and instantly he came to call. I suppose he saw his new home with us as a new beginning.

I am sure the spirit of his previous owner, the elderly lady, guided him to the salon that day, as I cannot imagine life without him now. I think when animals come to you, it's just meant to be.

Lots of people don't realise that animals can be really strong-minded, with a clear idea of what they do and do not want to do. One reading I did proved to me that some animals know exactly what they want.

Mr Jangles was a beautiful lemon sorbet-coloured pony. He shared his barn with two other ponies and a donkey. His two pony friends were extremely clever top-grade show jumpers; the donkey was a companion for Mr Jangles when the two ponies were away at shows at weekends. Mr Jangles' owners had asked me to come along to see if I could get to the bottom of his attitude problem. They had bought him as a show pony for their young daughter. She was only nine years old and a stroppy pony was proving very difficult to manage. They explained that when they took him in the arena at home, he became sluggish and refused to co-operate. Even worse, if they took him to a show, he started off well, then completely lost interest in what he was supposed to be doing and behaved utterly disgracefully, bucking and rearing.

His owners had checked all the obvious problems. They had back specialists out to check that his saddle fitted, dentists to check his teeth, farriers to check his feet and so on. They had spent an absolute fortune on him, and when all the specialists confirmed that everything was fine, they had no choice but to consider selling him. That's when they heard about me, and called me in as a last resort.

Mr Jangles was not amused when I arrived at his barn. In fact, he seemed so unhappy that it took me at least twenty minutes to connect with him.

I introduced myself when I finally got through to him, and tried to achieve some sort of two-way conversation.

'What's wrong? Why are you so unhappy?' I asked him.

'Them,' he said sharply.

'Do you mean the humans that look after you?' I asked.

'He is OK, but the others won't listen,' he said sadly.

I assumed by 'he' he meant the dad of the family, who didn't really have anything to do with the ponies except at feeding times and when driving the horse lorry to shows.

'Why not, Mr Jangles? What don't you like?'

'They won't listen,' he said again.

I translated what he was telling me and his owners were baffled, because they were kind people who tried their hardest to make Mr Jangles' life as happy as it could be.

I asked him what his owners needed to hear. And what they could do to help him.

'I want to jump like the other ponies,' he said.

I relayed this to his owners, but they said it was impossible as he was a show pony, which meant all feet on the ground and no jumps. They also mentioned that he had never jumped anything before as he was bred for showing. But Mr Jangles insisted he wanted to jump. So the only option was to make a compromise.

He suddenly sent me a picture of some jump fences. They weren't the usual coloured jumps you see in a showjumping arena. These were made of reeds, and were very natural and earthy. I relayed what I saw to his owners.

'That's working hunter,' the young girl said to her mother.

Mr Jangles swung round, with his ears pricked up.

'That's it!' he said to me, nuzzling my pockets for Polos.

It turned out he had seen other ponies jumping at the shows and really wanted to be one of them. So his owners agreed that he could try the working hunter class, which is a showing class with small natural brush jumps. Mr Jangles was thrilled with this, and agreed to behave himself if he were allowed to jump. Everyone was happy, so I left the yard happy too.

A couple of weeks later I heard from Mr Jangles' owners. They could hardly contain their excitement. Mr Jangles had turned out to be a brilliant jumping pony. At the first qualifying show of the season, Rebecca the daughter and Mr Jangles went into a working hunter class and had a near-perfect round. Mr Jangles never put a foot wrong, and they won. Not only that, but they qualified for the Horse of the Year Show. What a result! I was thrilled. They told me Mr Jangles was so very happy now and there was no way they would ever sell him. All it took was a small compromise. It turned out well for all involved.

After working for a few years with lots and lots of amazing animals, my work as an animal communicator was beginning to get noticed and I was also running very successful one-day workshops, teaching other people how to communicate with animals. At every workshop I was answering the same questions, over and over:

'How did you get started?'

'Have you always been able to hear the animals?'

'What have been your psychic experiences?'

I decided it would be a great idea to write my experiences down as a book, and after some thought I realised that the story of my life might also be of interest to some people. Maybe they would be able to relate to my world; maybe it would help them make sense of their own psychic experiences.

So I began to write. I realised I couldn't just send the book to a publisher, but first needed to find an agent to represent me. How and where would I find one? I had no idea. And it had to be an agent who works with my type of subject. Not an easy thing to achieve: would they think I was mad? I had watched a documentary about J. K. Rowling and *Harry Potter* and the presenter mentioned that the book had been turned down by many publishers, until one of them finally had the guts to take it on. The rest, as you know, is history. This just made me more determined to find the right agent.

I searched through lots of different sites on the internet for information on book submissions. I found about four agents that suited my style of book, and eagerly sent off the first three chapters I had written. I waited patiently for a response and, after just a few weeks, I was delighted to receive an encouraging email from one of the agents I'd contacted. Before I knew what was happening, I had been invited to London to discuss my little book.

Luckily for me, the agent who was interested in what I had written was a lovely, jolly man called Luigi. He sat behind his desk with a laptop in front of him, surrounded by lots of paperwork, and I sat on the sofa. I told him what the rest of the book would be about and he explained to me what publishing the book would mean. I was listening intently to what he was saying when I looked up at the bookshelves. Oh my God! I couldn't believe what I was seeing. The shelves were full of books written by top celebrities, everyday household names, people we all admire on TV. And there I was, the girl from 'Beduff', sinking deeper and deeper into the sofa in Luigi's office. I began to feel a little insecure. Why on earth would a top literary agent be interested in my life story? It was unreal.

Then to top it all, Luigi told me that he worked alongside a very good friend who looked after those celebrities for TV. Luigi wanted me to meet the owner of the company and so I nervously agreed to come back the following week to be introduced to Annie the

TV agent. Shaking Luigi's hand as I left the office that day was a moment I will never forget. It felt like a handshake that would change my future irrevocably.

A week later, I returned for the meeting with Annie, as planned. I was so nervous, shaking my head in disbelief that this could actually be happening to me. She was everything I admire: strong, direct and well groomed. I liked her instantly. She had perfectly styled blonde hair, pretty pink lips and what looked like a beautifully tailored Chanel suit.

We chatted long and hard, myself, Annie and Luigi. I had brought Fraser's mum Wilma along for support and she sat looking on in bewilderment. I couldn't believe how well things had turned out. I'd taken pot luck on the internet, and then met two of the most impressive people who could help me realise my dream of spreading the message about animal communication. I was totally flattered. The meeting went really well. They obviously had big ideas about my future and I was happy to go along with them. I agreed to everything and looked forward to what was in store for me and my book.

Writing this chapter feels unreal to me. It had been a complete fluke that I met Luigi my literary agent and then Annie the TV agent, the two people who would shape my media presence. I'm only me. I'm nothing special – just a real girl trying to make a difference in the world of animals and their owners. But I was swept along with the excitement of London and all it has to offer.

Before I knew what was happening, I had a lovely girl in Annie's office looking after my TV career. Her name is Fiona, and she is young, enthusiastic and very nice to me. I like working with her. She sorts out all the boring stuff, such as travel details and hotels, and she makes sure I'm looked after. I owe her a huge thank you.

I had been booked to go on Matthew Wright's show on Channel 5 as an animal expert, alongside a well-known Australian TV vet. We were to have some animals in the studio with their owners, and answer questions on the telephone. The whole animal bit was going to last between fifteen and twenty minutes. I've never been to drama school or had acting lessons and I'm obviously new to the TV world, so they must have been anxious when my debut was on a live show. But they trusted my ability as an animal communicator and let me run with it.

The day before the show I flew down to London to prepare. It was about 2pm and I was booked to see my literary agent for a quick meeting at 2.30. I live in the countryside at home and I find London a little scary. It always seems so bright and exciting, and very busy. As I walked up the road near the office, I felt slightly out of touch with reality. Everywhere I looked I saw trendy people, talking on their mobiles, chatting to friends, looking at ease. The odd American tourists caught my eye: they were so intrigued by the statues, the pigeons and our British way of life.

I wondered if anyone could see how scared I was. Could they see what I was about to embark on, and would they realise how out of touch, uncool and untrendy I was feeling? I'm a lot older than when I was dancing as a young girl with a gorgeous curvy size 14 figure to be proud of! Now, I'm a cuddly size 18 and the fake tan, high heels and glamour are all long gone. I suddenly felt fat and a bit awkward. But then I thought, Bugger, I am me! They will just have to accept me for who I am.

Being slightly early and nervous about meeting Luigi again, I decided to get a coffee from a shop next to the office. I smiled at the waiter and he started to reel off a million different drinks to choose from.

'Er, just coffee, please,' I stumbled.

He looked at me blankly. Oh, crikey! I am so uncool. I looked back just as blankly at him. At home it's just coffee. Instant or filter, if you're lucky. My attention was suddenly drawn to the chalkboard above the space-age coffee machine which looked like it could take you back in time with the push of a button. There were more knobs on it than a bed post.

'Latte, please. Yes, I'll have a latte,' I said confidently. Phew! I never realised getting a coffee could be so complicated. I smiled to myself as I left the coffee shop: it turned out a latte was just a normal coffee made with milk. Maybe I am not so behind the times after all, because when I was about nine years old, my mum and I used to go to the little café at Nuneaton bus station and I always ordered a milky coffee. So as it happens I probably invented it. They just changed the name.

Oops! Now I was going to be late, so I quickly finished my latte (or milky coffee to you and me) and made it to my appointment in the nick of time. Sitting in Luigi's office, I heard him say, 'So, Annie has got you on *The Wright Stuff* tomorrow morning?'

I nodded, trying to seem calm. 'Yes. Do you think it will be OK?' I asked, feeling terrified inside.

'No matter what happens, Joanne, just smile, smile, smile. Be yourself and smile!' he answered in a jolly voice.

Um, I thought. Great advice! But I laughed and took it on board.

Before I knew it I was at my hotel and ready for bed. I felt so lonely, but incredibly excited. I was about to show people how this work can actually be done. No one was more surprised than me when I woke to the alarm at 6am. I had slept very well, all night. And no nerves!

Then the phone call came from Fiona. 'Hi, Joanne. How are you this morning? Just to let you know the vet is not going to be on today, which means you will be doing the show on your own. You'll be fine.' And then she was gone.

Aghh! Bloody hell, no! On my own? Oh, I feel sick.

'You can do this, Joanne,' a little voice said in my head. Well, if I couldn't then I'd just smile, smile, smile.

The car arrived and I was taken to the studio. Trying not to look star-struck, I headed into the green room. (It's not green. It's just a place where you sit and wait to be called onto the set.) The room had lovely soft sofas, a coffee table with lots of that day's newspapers all arranged neatly into a fan shape, a couple of TVs and a bowl of fruit. Very nice, I thought to myself. Feeling a little out of sorts, I thought I would eat a piece of fruit to calm my nerves. With an apple in my mouth, I nearly choked when I saw the celebrities walk into the room. Oh my God! There in front of me were people off the telly. Was this real? Was I really here? I was awestruck.

Anyway, the show was live and so was I. And we were having a great time. We had three live animals on the couch with their owners – a small dog, a cat and a reptile – and three on TV screens above us. There was a guy who prompted the audience to clap at the right time, which they all seemed to enjoy doing, and different cameramen who scuttled across the floor getting the right camera angles. I didn't really notice the lights but I am sure there would have been a lot. My focus was totally on the animals.

When the red light on the camera went on, I was to look ahead and chat to the owner of the animal. I found it slightly weird, but I really didn't have any nerves. I adored working live with the animals. Each animal chatted to me freely and I was completely at ease. Each owner validated my information and everything I said went out with no editing, just the truth. At the end of the show I was allowed to read out five tips to camera for the audience at home on how they could communicate with their own animals. I thought this was brilliant. What a fantastic idea!

I remember the producer saying they had a huge number of phone calls about my work and they were thrilled at the response from the public. Matthew thanked me for being on the show and I must have looked like I was on energy drinks because I was totally buzzing. A chauffeur drove me to the train station and as soon as I was out of the car my mobile phone was ringing, 'Joanne,' my mum screamed down the phone, 'you were wonderful. I am so proud of you!'

'Mum, it was easy. The animals worked for me. I just listened. It was brilliant!' I felt tears come to my eyes. I had done it. I had finally got animal communication on mainstream TV. I couldn't wait to get back on.

For the following hour I was on and off my mobile to Fraser, Janice, Lyn, Yvonne and lots of other friends and family. I felt like a star! And I liked the feeling. But

I have to say the animals were the stars that day. They were truly amazing. The day went so well that I was asked back and I was on the show for nearly a year, doing my little slot on the couch with Matthew every five weeks. I loved it.

I was lucky enough to be asked to do various other shows, where I met some incredible people. When I was a guest on Sharon Osbourne's show, I got to chat with Minnie her little dog and Sophia the camel. Minnie told me some interesting personal stuff about Sharon, which she may not have wanted the world to know. All I know is, a lot more was said than was revealed on the show. Editing really is a bugger. They seem to like the fluffy side for TV, and not the gritty truth.

As for the camel, she was enormous! And very imposing up close. I have to admit I was a little scared. The stage wasn't that big, and Sophia had already taken off with her handler a couple of times that day. I was reading Sophia live in front of a huge studio audience when, sure enough, she became uncontrollable for a minute and, with a determined look in her eye, nearly pulled her handler to the floor. The problem was that Sharon and I were only about three feet away from this giant, and directly in her escape path. I looked at Sharon, she looked at me, and we both clung to each other in a fit of laughter and panic. OK, maybe I clung on more, but nevertheless, it was really funny that an animal communicator should be terrified of a camel. The audience found it hysterical. But I am sure I was quickly forgiven as my information was confirmed when chatting to her owner. But I will never forget that day. It was so much fun, even if it was slightly embarrassing. I'm laughing as I write this, and I am quite sure those of you who saw that show are too! You know what they say: never work with animals . . . Well, I'm stuffed then, eh?

I have always been treated really well on shows even though some of the presenters or producers are probably sceptics. They always allow me to be who I am and do what I'm good at. TV is a great platform to show people that communication with animals is possible, and the more you do, the more you get asked to do, which is great. I'm still unknown to most people, but I'm doing my little bit for the animals. In my family, I am known as the official Z-lister! (And that reminds me of Justin, a friend of the family who often takes the mickey out of my Z-lister status. He has an amazing cross Bengal cat called Ben who came to one of my workshops and spent most of the morning under a bush in the gardens of the hotel, refusing to come out. Very embarrassing – a communicator who can't talk a cat out of a bush.)

Although I prefer to do live shows if possible, I am truly grateful for everything I get asked to do. I especially love doing charity shows. *Only Fools on Horses* and *Celebrity Scissorhands* were both really interesting, but my biggest pleasure was being on *The Weakest Link Paranormal Special*. Anne Robinson is so not scary – in fact, she was lovely. It was a fabulous day. I took my sister Janice with me, and we were both treated like celebrities. We were awestruck as the other contestants came into the green room: Derek Acorah, one of my favourite psychics, Mia Dolan, Sally Morgan, the lovely Michele Knight and loads more. Wow! And then, later in the day, Mr Amazing himself, Gok! We are both fans of his fashion shows and were so excited to be seeing him in the flesh. We grinned at him like two crazy ladies, and he probably thought we were both nuts. The day was fantastic and yes, though I'm cringing as I write this, I was officially the weakest link. I am embarrassed about this, but I suppose someone had to go first. We raised over £13,000 for charity that day and, weakest link or not, I'd do it all over again, given the chance.

By now my career path was heading in the right direction. I had gone from being a little girl skipping up the path at Mavor Drive, Bedworth, to sitting on the sofa live on TV with Matthew Wright. Somehow it didn't seem real. I am normal. People like me don't end up on TV. Or so I thought. But here I was, being propelled from one show to the next, staying in spectacular hotels, being chauffeur-driven to studios and loving every minute. Who wouldn't? It's what dreams are made of. However, my feet are still firmly on the ground. I love all the good media, and it's all about spreading the word that communication with animals is actually possible. Through the media I am able to show more and more people about our work, and, in doing so, help more and more animals.

Chapter Eleven

As I sit here writing, I feel sad that this book has nearly come to an end. My emotions have never been so exposed, but it has been therapeutic, and a major turning point in my own self-belief. I can see the links in my life that have eluded me until now, and which are continuing to make me who I am today.

I very nearly didn't finish the book. It was the passing of my little poodle Klein that spurred me on. He has played an important part in my life, along with my other angels with whiskers, and I felt this book would be one of the best ways to make sure he would never be forgotten. Sadly, he hasn't been the only animal friend I've lost. My lovely Mozart left us just as I thought everything was going great again.

Every day after work, I would come home, open the kennel door and let Mozart, Ruben and Rosie, my beautiful borzois, out to play. This normally led to Rosie and Ruben racing around like thunder, and Mozart catching up with them as and when he could. Mozart was still full of fun, and would wag his tail with a goofy look on his face, watching them whizz past him.

One day it was different. I was busy playing with the pups when I noticed Mozart sniffing the grass at the side of the wooded kennel.

'What you doin', Mozty?' I said in my funny voice that I only used for him. He loved it, and would often give me one of his cheesy grins.

Suddenly I had a gut feeling, a deep sense of sadness. Mozart turned and walked to the front of the garage, sat down and stared at me. I felt frozen in time, not able to move an inch. I looked at him, melting into his eyes. His expression was soft, but I was not prepared for what came next. I had put the possibility of communication with him behind me long ago.

'I'm ready,' he said. The voice was strong, clear and calm.

I began to shake and my eyes filled with tears of disbelief.

'No,' I whispered. 'No, this cannot be right.'

'I'm ready,' he said again, this time with a look that took my breath away.

I knew what he meant. He was ten years old, but he was fit and lively. He looked fine. There were no symptoms at all. But I knew exactly what he meant. I was in total shock. I ran into the house to tell Fraser what I had heard.

'Fraser!' I yelled.

'What's the matter?' Fraser jumped up off the couch, expecting the worst. 'What is it?'

I'm not sure what he was thinking, but I could see he was worried at the way I was looking.

'Mozart has just said he's ready!' I gasped.

'Ready? Ready for what?' he asked, confused.

'Ready to go, die, pass, leave us! Leave me!' I cried, tears streaming down my face.

'Hey, don't be silly. He is fine. He was out playing with the pups earlier today.' Fraser smiled.

Maybe I was wrong. Maybe it was all in my head. Maybe I had made it up, like every other communication, according to my sceptics. That was all Mozart said to me: nothing more, nothing less. But I knew.

The next day, I took Fraser's advice and put what I

had heard behind me. It had been a long day at work and I was looking forward to putting my feet up. Driving up to the top of the hill, no more than five minutes away from home, I received the phone call. It was Fraser.

'Come home quick. It's Mozart!' he said.

'What's happened?'

'He was in the garden, and just collapsed. He won't or can't move. Hurry!'

I arrived at the house within minutes, and there he was, flat out in front of me on the drive. Fraser had covered him with a blanket and kept talking to him. We carried Mozart into the kitchen (no easy feat, I can assure you, with such a huge borzoi) and laid him on a blanket. I looked into his eyes. It has never been clearer. 'I'm ready.'

I explained to Fraser what I was planning to do. Mozart and I were going to sleep together on the kitchen floor one last time. He wasn't in pain; he was just giving up. I phoned my vet and asked him to come out in the morning at eleven. But I thought he might not even last the night.

That night lying quietly on the kitchen floor together, lying, I cuddled him and he cuddled me back.

He wouldn't eat, drink or do anything but lie quietly by my side. I whispered all my love for him that night and I know that every word registered with him. At some point I fell asleep, and so too did Mozart. I woke up early the following morning, but I kept my eyes shut tight. I was really scared that if I opened them he would be dead. Then to my amazement I heard a low groan, as if he knew I was awake. When I opened my eyes, he was staring straight at me with those beautiful hazel eyes, so full of love but so ready to go. I kissed away his fears.

It wasn't long before my vet was at our side. He examined Mozart and totally agreed with my decision to help him on his way. It was heartbreaking. I held him and talked to him whilst the vet got the needle ready. It was time.

'I love you, Mozart. I'll always love you,' I whispered to him.

The vet lifted his paw and was just about to place the needle into the vein, when Mozart just slipped away, right in front of our eyes. He was gone. I nodded to the vet to carry on. He looked confused but I knew Mozart wanted a little help, and so that's what I needed to do.

I stayed with Mozart for a while before I prepared to take him to my friends and then we buried him alongside his best buddy Mosko. It was a really emotional day, but at last Mosko and Mozart were reunited on the top of a beautiful, peaceful hill.

Before Mozart passed to spirit, I occasionally came across people who just wouldn't or didn't accept that animals could really speak to us humans. They made me feel like a fake, telling me I was making it all up and accusing me of taking advantage of people. To be honest it was usually water off a duck's back, but my grief for Mozart affected me more than I realised; it was almost as if the sadness I felt had destroyed my normal defences against criticism. Now I began to feel that the pressure was too much. The work I loved was becoming strained, and I nearly gave up completely. I spent more and more time in the grooming salon and less time working on my communication. A feeling of loss came over me as it had before, when I was young. The feeling was familiar to me. Just as Paul had left a gaping hole in my heart, so too did Mozart.

I confided in Yvonne, my friend and colleague.

'Yvonne, I don't think I can do this any more,' I said.

'Joanne, you have to. You have a gift, and you have a duty to use it,' she replied.

'It's just too hard. There are too many sceptics trying to rubbish my work. It's beginning to make me wonder if it's all in my head,' I said.

'Joanne, you heard Mozart didn't you? Do it for him. The animals need you.'

I remembered those words – 'I'm ready' – and I felt a shockwave run through my body.

'Yes, I did hear him, and all of the others!'

What on earth was I thinking? By now I had done hundreds of successful readings. And not only that, I had taught lots of other people how to hear their animals. Bloody hell, Joanne, get a grip, I thought to myself. It's funny, isn't it: a hundred people can be pleased with your work, and then one person comes along and tells you it's not real, and suddenly you can only hear those words. I was not going to let anyone put me off. I was on a mission!

I was glad that communication enabled me to hear Mozart in his final hours. My communication skills had been validated once and for all, and I knew I would carry on and spread the word that this was one hundred per cent real. I had heard him, loud and clear.

My grief for Mozart was hard enough to take, but my next loss floored me. Why? Well, through everything that I have endured over the years – the sceptics, the ridicule, the lessons – no one has given me more passion to carry on than my little Klein.

Klein and I were together for nearly eighteen years, but I knew it couldn't last for ever. He was frail, slightly blind and a little deaf. He could still sniff out a piece of chicken a mile off, but he looked like the walking dead. Many people who saw him thought he should have been put out of his misery, but what they didn't understand was that I trusted my connection with him, I knew that when he was ready, he would let me know. Some days he was so very frail that I would beg him to pass over, but the tiger inside him wanted to carry on.

I had often fretted about what I'd do with him once he had passed. I could bury him in the garden, but what if we moved? We had never been apart and I would have to leave him behind. One Wednesday morning, I had a tremendous urge to go and find out about animal crematoriums. Yvonne had read an article about a lady called Dawn who offered pet crematorium services. So we went along to see her later that day, mainly to ask questions about what she offered.

We arrived at a very sweet Scottish cottage. We could see a variety of little animal-sized memorials in the front garden. It was really peaceful. Dawn answered the door and invited us into a quiet comfortable room. She explained that her service was to take care of your animal after it had died, taking it directly to the crematorium and making sure he or she was cremated with dignity and returned back to you the same day, either in a scatter box or in a specially designed ornamental urn.

This amazing lady helps people when they are at their lowest, taking the worry out of their hands and making sure their pet is safe right up to the end. She will even help people if their animal is going to be put to sleep at the vet's, being there with them for support and comfort no matter what they decide to do with the body afterwards.

I so admired her work, but felt I needed to take full control of Klein when the time came. So I asked her if this would be possible. It sounds morbid, but I couldn't bear to be parted from him. I wasn't expecting her to offer me the help she did, but Dawn told me about a lovely crematorium in Cumbria that she used, and said that I would be made welcome when the time came.

I felt at ease that evening, knowing that I had a plan at last, and I sat on the sofa and told Fraser all about it.

The next morning Klein woke me early. I couldn't believe what I was seeing. He was ready. I asked him to confirm and his answer was crystal clear. No chicken bribery was needed that day. He lay motionless. He wouldn't eat, drink or lift his head. His time had come. I will never forget that morning. Did he guide me to go and see Dawn the day before? Was it meant to be? I thought back to the reading of the terrier who knew she was going to die. Did Klein know too?

I dressed him in a soft grey fleece hoody that he loved to wear in cold weather as he grew older, and placed him in his favourite furry bed so he was warm and comfortable. We said our goodbyes through tears triggered by memories, good and bad, whilst waiting for the vet to arrive. Just like Mozart before him, Klein slipped peacefully away before the injection even went in. It was heartbreaking to see my boy pass over, but a strange relief, knowing he was ready. And knowing I had listened.

Yvonne and I drove two hours to the crematorium where I placed Klein into the furnace. It was a simple brick-built, enclosed dry square, with a metal door on the front. There were no flames, and I was re-assured by how peaceful it looked. I put him inside on his little bed and in his hoody, closed the door and said goodbye. This was something I needed to do, and the lady was very understanding. I needed to say goodbye and to know he was the only one in there. He was at rest.

We waited in the room at the back, which held memoirs of other animals that their owners had written. It was moving to know how much so many people love their animals. They really are so precious.

I chose a small wooden box, which had some white snowdrops painted on one side. I thought this was sweet because I'd noticed the streams of snowdrops covering the grass verges when we were driving into the village. Klein's ashes were placed into the box and I had a simple inscription put on the front, reading: Mr Klein – Daddy's little tiger. It was perfect. Klein and I would never have to be apart. His resting place is on our mantelpiece, watching over us all.

Today I take his memory with me wherever I go. He will live in my heart for ever, and every reading I do has his paw of approval. I have lost, I have loved and now I can help other people who are going through a similar experience to realise how lucky we are to have shared our lives with these remarkable furry balls of love.

I often get emails or letters from people asking for information from their pets who have passed over to spirit. I read lots of animals who were ill and have passed and are now healthy and happy on the other side. So is this the same connection as a psychic gets with human spirit? Or is it different for the animal kingdom? No, it's exactly the same! Just as you can get validation from living animals, you can also get validation from animals who have passed over. I feel this is a great way for us to heal. After losing a pet, we mourn the loss of a family member and friend, and it hurts so much. It's important to understand that although it is one of the most painful situations to be in with your loved animal, the truth is that they do live on.

One morning the owner of a big fat orange cat called Bradley rang me to explain that unfortunately he had passed over to spirit in his sleep. Bradley was a gorgeous cat. I had done a reading for him and his mum the previous year, which had helped them overcome some bonding issues. (Bradley was known for secretly jumping into other people's cars and ending up miles from home.)

'Oh, Gillian, I am sorry. He was a lovely cat,' I said in sympathy.

'I know. It was such a shock. He seemed fine yesterday,' she said.

'So what now? Are you going to bury him in your garden?' I asked.

All of a sudden I felt a tingle in my body. My focus was moving away from Gillian and being pulled to another.

'Hey, not the garden!' shouted a voice from beyond, a voice I recognised. It was Bradley.

'I was thinking . . .' Gillian was about to say more but I stopped her in mid-sentence.

'Gillian, hold on a moment. I think we have a visitor to our conversation.'

'What? Who?' she asked, slightly confused.

'It's me,' he said to me.

'Yes, Bradley. I know it's you, but your mum doesn't,' I laughed.

'Gillian, Bradley is with me.' I knew she wouldn't freak out because Gillian had been to one of my workshops in the past and so understood all about communicating with animals alive and dead.

'Tell him I love him,' she squealed in utter delight.

'I know,' he said.

'He says he knows,' I replied.

'Tell him he is my world,' she demanded.

'I know,' he replied.

'He knows!' I laughed.

Crikey! This conversation could take for ever, I thought to myself. For everyone's sake, I decided to ask Bradley if he needed to say goodbye or wanted to pass any messages on to Gillian.

'Do not bury me in that bloody garden,' he said with the sarcasm only a cat could manage.

I repeated what he had said to Gillian, and waited for her reply.

'Why?' she asked.

'I want to go travelling,' he said, in a matter of fact voice. 'I always liked travelling.'

He made me giggle. He did indeed like to travel. What a funny cat.

'Gillian, as we all know, he likes to travel, so I think it's probably best if you have him cremated and take his ashes to different places far and wide.'

'That's fantastic. My sister and I are going round the world next month. Good old Bradley can come too!'

And so Bradley was granted his wish. The three of them travelled all over the world, and whilst doing so Gillian scattered a little of his ashes in each country. What a lovely ending for such a lovely cat.

Catherine called me to see if I could help find her dog Pepsi, a small black, tan and white King Charles spaniel.

'She's gone Joanne, she's gone,' she cried.

'What do you mean gone?' I asked.

'Run away. She just ran!'

I got Catherine to explain what had happened the day Pepsi went, and it turned out they had been in the park near their home. Catherine took her eye off Pepsi for just a few seconds and that was that – her little dog had disappeared.

'It's not like her, Joanne. She is nearly seven years of age, and has never run off before,' she explained, struggling to catch her breath through her tears.

I began to feel a sensation, just as I always do when tuning into animals – the tingling, the focus. Wow, I thought. This is odd. It seemed too quick, and I felt a little weird because it was as if Pepsi was dead, a spirit dog, and not alive.

'Pepsi, is this you?' I asked in my head.

'Yes, it's Pepsi,' the little voice replied.

'Where are you? What can you hear? What can you see?'

'A tree. It smells funny,' the little dog said.

I was still getting a strange feeling of death surrounding this connection. It just didn't seem right at all.

'Pepsi, are you alive?' I asked.

'Yes,' she replied.

But something wasn't right, so I asked if she was with anyone.

'Yes,' she replied again.

Maybe she had been dog-napped? Now I was getting concerned.

Catherine was telling me about the day leading up to Pepsi's disappearance, from start to finish. She kept saying that Pepsi had been acting oddly, staring into corners at nothing, almost following shadows around her house. It was so out of character that she had booked an appointment with the vet for the following evening, just to make sure she was OK.

I asked Pepsi, 'Who are you with?'

'Angel,' she replied.

My heart sank. I had an awful feeling I knew what was coming next.

'Angel is here. We are together again.'

'Catherine,' I said, 'your other dog, what was her name again?'

I knew through friends of Catherine that she had owned two dogs, and that one of them had passed a month or two back, leaving Pepsi on her own. I needed to be clear on my information, and when Catherine replied, 'Angel,' I knew straightaway what this meant. Not good news. I could quite easily have told Catherine there and then what I heard from Pepsi, but sometimes tact is important. In this case, I felt the only way was to allow Catherine to find Pepsi for herself, with me guiding her to Pepsi's resting place.

'Catherine?' I said.

'Yes, Joanne? Are you getting anything? Are you picking up any information from Pepsi? Please say,' she begged.

'OK, I think I may know where Pepsi is,' I said, and asked Pepsi which way she had headed after she left her mum in the park. Catherine retraced Pepsi's steps as I relayed them to her on her mobile: past the line of trees on the left with the bird box on, then across a small footbridge towards the main road. Pepsi was answering each question clearly and in detail. I wasn't picturing the area at all; no, it was her little voice that was being translated to me, clear as daylight.

She had taken Catherine almost half a mile when I suddenly heard a scream down the phone line.

'Catherine, are you OK?'

But it was obvious she had found Pepsi. Her cries of grief were loud enough for anyone to hear.

'Joanne, I've found her,' she cried uncontrollably. 'She is dead!'

It was almost a relief to hear the words. Firstly, Catherine had found her body, but almost more importantly – to me at least – my feelings of a passing with this little dog had been confirmed. My job is sad at times. Sometimes the overwhelming grief I feel, not only for the animals but for the people as well, is hard to shoulder. But it's my job, and I have to learn from it, to grow and develop more skills to appreciate how utterly amazing animals can be, both living and passed.

Catherine found Pepsi's little body lying peacefully

under a tree, exactly where she had said she had seen a tree, and it smelt funny too, just as she had stated. There was a tray full of some sort of chemical under the tree. It looked like water but smelt horrid. As far as Catherine could tell, Pepsi hadn't drunk any, nor had she been attacked or run over. In fact, there were no obvious signs to show why she had died. But the vet and Catherine later put it down to a broken heart, from the grief of missing Angel. I like to think Angel came down to collect her sister so they could be together once more as they had been on earth. Inseparable.

On some occasions I have found that, when an animal passes suddenly, their residual energy may be left behind. I did a reading of a cat that had been poisoned by a neighbour; the distraught owner found his body at the end of the garden. After she buried the cat's body, strange things started happening around her house. She noticed her sofa had an indent as if something had been lying on it; she heard quiet meows, and scratching coming from various places around the house. Not understanding what this meant, the lady contacted me.

When I did a reading from a photograph, it turned out that the cat had no idea he was dead, so he carried on doing the things he had always done: meowing for food, scratching to get in, and sleeping on the sofa. My client was amazed! We decided it would be best if we explained to the cat what had happened and helped him pass to the world of spirit completely. After I completed the process, the owner soon noticed that the strange happenings had stopped. She was overwhelmed and very pleased that her cat was now at peace.

In my experience, animals not knowing they have passed can happen if the animal has had an unexpected death, such as being hit by a car or, as in the case above, being poisoned. In some cases, I have heard them say, 'I didn't see the car.' They have died instantly, but carried on in their spirit body like nothing has happened.

In my work as a communicator, I often get called to help animals face the end of their lives with dignity and grace. No matter how many times it happens, I still find it difficult to deal with animals passing to spirit. It never gets easier and leaves me exhausted and emotional for weeks after. One such client was an Old English mastiff who was very old and in terrible pain with arthritis. Her human mum Mavis knew that the time was coming when she would have to say goodbye to her dear friend, but she just couldn't bear to face it alone.

I arrived at her house early one morning and was shown into a side sitting room. The walls were covered with artefacts from all over the world. Mavis had been a keen traveller in her younger days, and had collected many beautiful objects for her home. We sat opposite each other on the huge cushioned sofas and she explained that Lady, her dog and best friend, was ready to go to spirit. She said she didn't want to be on her own at this time because she thought her family just would not understand her grief. Mavis asked if I would help Lady pass, alongside the vet. I agreed and we made our way through to the other room at the back of the house.

Mavis had arranged for the vet to arrive at noon that day, so we set about preparing Lady's departure from this world into the next. Now, sometimes this can be as simple as sitting with your pet. But in Mavis's case, she wanted the room and Lady's surroundings to represent her spirit. We had soft Indian music playing in the background, and burning sticks filled the room with exotic scents. There were lots of extra large crushed velvet burgundy cushions for Lady to rest her head and body on, helping her feel as comfortable as she could.

At this point Lady was lying quite still. She was relaxed and there was absolutely no question that she was ready for her final stage of life. She had held on for weeks, but Mavis just hadn't been able to let her go. I find this happening quite often in my work: the animals will hang on and on until their owners are ready to let go. So I was relieved that the day had come and Lady would finally be free of her crippling conditions.

Mavis and I sat for a few minutes and I held her hand as she said her final goodbyes to Lady. It was extremely emotional. They had been best friends and companions, so the loss was a tough one to accept. Then I talked Lady through what was going to happen when the vet arrived. I told her that she wasn't to be scared, everything would be just fine and Mavis would be right by her side. I knew she could hear every word, but I needed to make sure she was ready.

'Lady, do you wish for the vet to help you pass to spirit?' I whispered.

'Yes,' the frail voice replied.

That was all I needed. One of the worst things that can happen to animals is that they are put to sleep and actually they are not ready to go at all. This happens so very often, and I always ask the animal the question and advise people to do the same. The animals will always answer you clearly at this time.

The vet arrived and sat down next to Mavis and Lady.

'Hello, old gal. You will be running free and happy very soon,' he said warmly to Lady.

'Are you ready, Mavis?' he asked her gently.

Tears were streaming down her face as I put my arm around her shoulders to comfort her. This was now my time to visualise Lady happy and content, sending loving images to her as she said her last goodbye.

'Tell Mum I love her, and thank you,' she said as she breathed in a final breath, and then she was gone.

I relayed Lady's message to Mavis, and she leant down and kissed Lady on the forehead. 'Thank you, my sweet. Thank you for touching my heart.'

It was a very emotional time, but a strange peace came over the house. Lady was free. And Mavis was able to say goodbye to her friend with dignity.

Today, with just my beautiful borzoi Rosie sharing my life, I've been turned from a traditional dog family to a new style cat family, featuring Oshan, the very handsome sealpoint Siamese who has the deepest blue eyes; Vegas, the beautiful white Persian I rescued; Puss Puss, the little raggedy piebald moggy who came to me for help; and my newest addition Chana, my super flashy jet black Oriental showgirl: she's sleek, seductive and rules the roost! I never thought I'd be the carer of such wonderful animals. Cats are so very intuitive. They always know what I'm thinking, so maybe they should be known as human psychics!

Life is good. I am now thirty-eight years old. Fraser and I are happier than ever and I have reached a place from which I can look back and thank God for every opportunity (good and bad) and for the incredible animals I have had the pleasure of working with. No matter what the weather outside, my heart is full of sunshine, full of the warmth of people's love for their animals.

I've made mistakes in my life, as we all do at some point, and I am sure I will make some more. After all, I am a mere human. But every mistake is a lesson: I wouldn't be who I am today without them. I believe it is part of the process of self-discovery, for if I was perfect there would be nothing to improve. And improvement and education is key to my work. My strength is to teach what I know, so my future will be looking forward, helping new communicators to develop and celebrating the amazing psychic connections we have with the animals.

Even after years of being a professional pet sychic, I still have days of insecurity about my readings, but I am learning new things about the animals every day, such as how astonishingly complex they can be in their relationships, or how even the scariest of creatures that make the hairs on my arms stand up and my throat tighten with pure fear are actually full of love and warmth. The animals never cease to amaze me. I have been blessed with exciting work, and I know that I will be able to touch a few more hearts and help some more of the beautiful animals that are my world.

Just one more note before I leave. I am nobody special. I am still that little girl who loved Blackie so much. Maybe I'm older and wiser now, but I'm an ordinary girl who has been lucky enough to have been blessed with the knowledge of animal communication. It is not a special gift that only I possess: this is a gift that everyone can have – if they want it . . .

To love is to listen; to listen is to love.

With love,

Joanne x

Acknowledgements

So many people encouraged me to write this book: I would like to thank you all for your belief in me.

A big thank you from the bottom of my heart to my agent Luigi Bonomi, who always had faith in me, and to my publishers Headline and their team, especially my editors Carly Cook and Josh Ireland who helped me make sense of it all.

Thank you to my precious Blackie for his protection and love whilst I was growing up. And to my amazing mum Jean and dad Larry for their constant support in everything I do. To Jan, my fantastic sister who shares my belief in all that is unbelievable! And Rich, my brother, who is a sceptic but still loves to hear what I've been up to.

To the rest of my family, Judith, Julie, Ashlee, Shannon, Billy, Kerry and Laura, and the wonderful people in all walks of life who continue to strive for a better life for the innocent animals – you will always be my inspiration. To Fraser my wonderful, long-suffering fiancé. You have been my rock for nearly twelve years, being my one constant support through the good and bad times, I love you. And to his mum and dad Wilma and Jim – who believed in my dream of writing this book. Yvonne and Lyn, my best friends, for their unconditional friendship. And Uncle John's beautiful dog Troy, and Minnie the cat for being the most fabulous cover stars for this book.

And, of course, thank you to the animals: without them this book would not have been possible.

Last but not least, my thanks go to Mr Klein, the little toy poodle with whom I spent nearly eighteen years of my life, for cuddling me when I was sad, being my friend when I was lonely and making my time with him so very precious. I will love you for ever. x

Joanne's passion is to teach other people how to communicate with animals in workshops which she runs nationally and internationally. A new 12 Module Home Study Course is also available. Please see her website for more details and forthcoming events: www.joannehull.com